THE PUBLIC WORSHIP OF GOD

J. R. P. SCLATER

D0778213

THE PUBLIC WORSHIP
OF GOD

BEING THE LYMAN BEECHER LECTURES
ON PRACTICAL THEOLOGY AT YALE, 1927

BY

J. R. P. SCLATER

BAKER BOOK HOUSE
Grand Rapids, Michigan

Reprinted 1970 by Baker Book House Company
Standard Book Number: 8010-7914-4

PRINTED IN THE UNITED STATES OF AMERICA

Notable Books on Preaching

Among the helps for the minister and the theological student are the many volumes on preaching and homiletics. On our shelves are the single volumes written by individual men. There are well known series of lectures, such as the Yale or Lyman Beecher given at Yale Divinity School, New Haven, and the Warrack given to the four University Theological colleges in Scotland. Not many today possess full sets of these famous lectures. Earlier works are unobtainable as they are out of print and some cease to appeal. Nevertheless, the preacher who has access to this thesaurus of preaching and homiletics finds much to suggest and stimulate. Because of this, the time is opportune to select and reissue some of the books which have stood the test of time and have proved of abiding value.

It is proposed to issue a selection over the next few years. Not all will be alike. The homiletical techniques will be observed in them, but the emphases will vary. The wisdom and experience of those who have labored in other days may prove of lasting value in many a difficult hour. The particular books have been chosen in the belief that each will minister to the preacher in different moods of the soul. Representative of those which will be selected are:

The Sermon, by R. C. H. Lenski

The Preacher, His Life and Work, by J. H. Jowett

In Christ's Stead, by A. J. Gossip

The Building of the Church, by C. E. Jefferson

The Preacher and his Models, by J. Stalker

Jesus Came Preaching, by George Buttrick

Lectures on Preaching, by Phillips Brooks

The Glory of the Ministry, by A. T. Robertson

"Preaching can never lose its place so long as the mystery and wonder of the human spirit remain" is the judgment of Charles Sylvester Horne, *The Romance of Preaching.* Believing in the supremacy of preaching as God-appointed for the Church, the minister must equip himself for an incredible task of service. One of the causes of failure in the ministry lies in the lack of definite reading and study. These books will serve to spur on the preacher to greater deeds. We need not copy any man, but we can learn from all who have blazed the trail before us. "Who keeps one end in view, Makes all things serve" (R. Browning).

In issuing these volumes it is our hope and prayer that they will help to keep the ideals fresh and the standards from sagging while the vision remains clear. We must "plod on and keep the passion fresh."

RALPH G. TURNBULL

The First Presbyterian Church
of Seattle, Washington

Introduction

John Robert Paterson Sclater (1876-1949)
The Public Worship of God

Sclater is remembered for his pastorates in Derby, England; Edinburgh, Scotland; and two churches in Toronto, Canada: Parkdale and Old St. Andrews.

He was the preacher-scholar, a man of wide and deep reading. His preparation for the pulpit was thorough. His method was to make careful sermon outlines or full notes, photograph them in his memory, and then preach freely after brooding over these. Usually he could recapture the message from the outline and thus be free in gesture and contact with his congregation.

Evidently he was a man of artistic temperament and a lover and student of the best literature. He was grounded in theology and church history, and had a special feeling for the conduct of public worship with reverence and devotion. Standing in the holy place he preached in the grand tradition of his generation.

This book comprises material given under the Warrack lectures and then under the Yale lectures — an honor given to few in sharing in both. He delivered these in the same way as he preached — without notes — and then wrote his manuscript afterwards.

The book is suggestive in its spirit, dealing with the total hour of worship and its many-sided details. The sermon is not signalled out alone, but is set within the context of all aspects of public worship. We sense the love of the beautiful in the preacher's life and ministry. To him worship was the highest end of the soul. To lead people to the heights was his aim and his words will inspire all who read and mark well.

RALPH G. TURNBULL

PREFACE

When the invitation came to me to deliver the Lyman Beecher lectures, a familiar quotation came into my mind and remained there,—*sutor, ne supra crepidam:* and I determined that this cobbler, at any rate, would endeavour to stick to his last. After all, the purpose of the lectureship can well be served, when a working minister frankly speaks out of his own experience and explains, as best he can, the methods which he has found effective in practice. The work of the ministry has mostly to be done by the rank and file: and it is, perhaps, not unseemly that one of their own number should have an opportunity of discoursing upon the problems he has met and has tried to solve.

These particular lectures (except the last one) were delivered *extempore,* with only rare references to notes; and I have not found it possible entirely to recapture them in book form. Consequently, certain passages have been omitted altogether, especially in the chapters on prayer and preaching. In the lectures, I ventured to give practical examples of the disastrous results of haphazard and careless methods of preparation and delivery—examples which lose their force unless illustrated alike by voice and gesture. For the rest, however, the book follows closely the content, if not the manner, of the spoken addresses.

While, in work of this kind, a man draws for the most part from his own experience, it is inevitable that he should be indebted also to previous writers. An article by Dr. Stalker on preaching suggested the passage dealing historically with the art; and three of the quotations in the last chapter were drawn from Dr. Moffat's "Literary Illustrations of the Bible." But one apparent source of inspiration was not, in point of fact, known to me, until the lectures were complete. Readers of Dr. Sperry's "Reality in Worship" will notice an extraordinary similarity between some of the ideas in chapter one of this book, and those that are to be found in a corresponding chapter of Dr. Sperry's work. He, I notice, remarks a further correspondence in Dr. Vogt's "Art and Religion." I can only say that these lectures were finished before I had read

either of these books—though I have studied
them both since with delight and profit.

Any indebtedness that I owe, in this region,
is to a teacher of the previous generation. In the
chapter on prayer, I have paid a tribute to
the influence and example of the late Principal
Oswald Dykes of Westminster College, Cam-
bridge. It is to that fine student of all things
worshipful that I, and many others also, owe any
sensitiveness to devotional seemliness that we
possess. In particular, the scheme of the meanings of the Sacrament in chapter six is based on
a scheme which Dr. Dykes used for instructing
catechumens. I have altered it somewhat; and,
for the form of its explanation, I am entirely responsible. Nevertheless, the original suggestion
came from him. I had his permission to make
what use of it I would; and, during all my ministry, I have founded upon it when teaching the
meaning of the Holy Communion.

Chapters three, four and five contain work that
was done some years ago, when I had the privilege of holding the Warrack Lectureship on
Preaching, in Scotland. And that leads me to
record the real debt which any working minister,
who lectures on worship, must owe, but can never

pay. His true teachers are his people. They
endure his mistakes; they encourage him to do his
best; and by their friendship and loyalty help
him to grow. I have been minister of four
churches. First in Derby, then in Edinburgh,
then in Parkdale, Toronto, and now in my present charge. I found kindliness in them all. Indeed, young ministers may take heart. Their
work will bring them in touch with the best that
is in people; and they will be able to thank God
upon every remembrance of them. Most of my
working life, however, has been spent in the second of these—in the New North Church of Edinburgh, with all its memories of students and of
friendship rich and rare. The members of that
church, and especially those who worked inti-
mately in it, will allow me here to remember with
unfading affection "the friends I lo'ed sae weel
sae lang ago."

To my present congregation (which I like to
link with the New North) I am equally indebted.
They, also, are friends indeed. In particular,
thanks are due to my secretary, Miss Elsie Watt,
for indefatigable and very competent assistance,
and to my colleague, Dr. J. E. Munro, and Miss
Agnes Swinarton for reading the final proofs.

One thing about the ministry is that there are always willing folk about, ready to lend a helping hand. There is a great deal of sheer kindness in this world; and we ministers get our fair share. At any rate, one "poor brother" has found that true in Scotland, and finds it true now in Canada; and endeavours to give God the praise.

J. R. P. SCLATER.

Old St. Andrew's Church,
Toronto, Canada.

CONTENTS

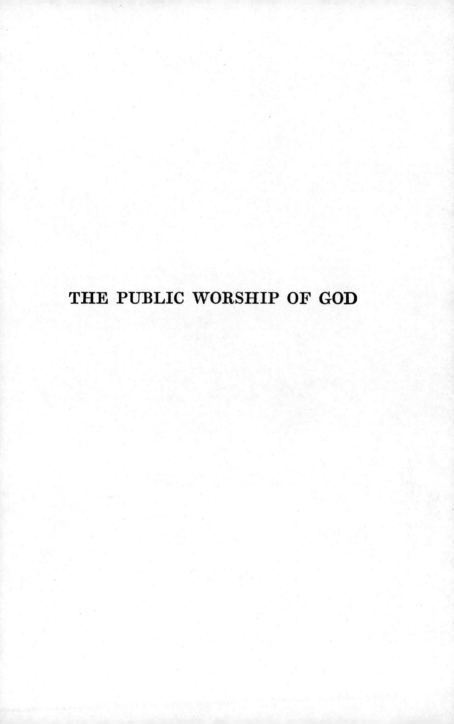

THE PUBLIC WORSHIP OF GOD

THE PUBLIC
WORSHIP OF GOD

CHAPTER I.

THE ORDER OF WORSHIP.

THE public worship of God is the concern of
every man. Both those who share in it and
those who do not, are enriched by its reality and
reverence, or impoverished by its lack of them.
For it is the chief of all the ordinary means for
keeping alive the sense of the Unseen in the community. The weekly services of the Church, on
a day traditionally set apart for them, have an
effect on society beyond that which they exercise
upon the actual worshippers. The church bell,
and the sight of families wending their way to
the sanctuary, are not without influence upon
those whom Sunday calls only to somnolence or
golf. Cases are not unknown of men, who
normally acknowledge God by proxy, waxing
vigourous in defence of weekly worship, and even

joining in it, if they feel that the practice is in
danger. For they know full well that, at least,
it keeps a window open to Jerusalem in their
children's hearts—and even, it may be, in their
own.

If public worship is to render all the service it
can to society, its component parts need to be dis-
cerned, that none may be omitted. The object
of this great act is, of course, God Himself; but
the worshipper is man—whose sole endeavour, at
such a moment, should be to present himself as
he really is, before his Maker. Consequently,
times of worship are occasions when man is
brought face to face with himself, and reminded
of the large, pathetic facts of his own life. They
afford almost the only ordinary opportunities for
him to take a steady look at the mystery, which
is himself. In business he has no time to remember: in pleasure, his anxiety is to forget.
Few men, apart from the hours of worship, ever
stand at gaze before the facts of birth and death,
before their own pitifulness and splendour, their
transience and their permanence. Yet all men
know that it is only those who take thought upon
these things, who grow in wisdom. And it is no
small service that the Church renders, in a world

of shadows and the pursuit of shadows, when it affords opportunity to behold the tears of things and to touch the trappings of mortality, and thus to move upwards to the place where the Eternal dwells.

Hence, no apology, surely, is needed for beginning with a consideration of the best means of arranging services which have so deep a significance. Indeed, it is a comfort to observe the interest that is being shown in all our Reformed Churches, in the matter of a proper Order of Service. The ancient fears, that due arrangement and preparation of worship savour of the Pope or of Black Prelacy, have been largely assuaged: and all our branches of the Church are engaged in the production of service books, which purport to be guides to ministers and congregations. Some of us have observed with delight what attention our people are willing to give to discussions of the ascending scale of meanings, which a rightly ordered act of worship ought to possess. Moreover, the unlovely has had its day and tawdriness is following it into banishment. Squat ugliness is no longer regarded as a mark of spirituality; nor is it thought necessary to be formless in order not to be formal. These are happier days for all who care for beauty of expression. Perhaps it is a reaction from the war: but more men care for loveliness than was the case a quarter of a century ago.

But a situation of that sort is full of danger. In the rebound from the bare, it is easy to fall into the meaningless. In practice, the "beautifying" of our services often means the introduction of responses or of music, which have no relation to a concerted act of worship; just as the "decorations" which are splashed about our walls have no relation to the fact that they are the walls of a church. Indeed, some modern "beautiful" services are more distressing than the stern worship that had a loveliness of its own, because it sought none. For these old services possessed a unity peculiar to themselves. They proposed worship through the mind, with no appeal to the senses at all; while their modern successors, by ranging aimlessly up and down the gamut of religious expression, lose unity, and thus the first condition of beauty.

Consequently, all ministers need to give time and thought to the structure of their services. In making the suggestions that follow, I have particularly in mind those, who, being of the Puritan and Covenanting lineage, find themselves in congregations, which have not much of this world's gear, and cannot command the services of first-rate musicians or erect churches of architectural distinction. Some books that have recently appeared contain admirable guidance for parishes inhabited by millionaires. But most men work amongst poor folk and inherit buildings in which ornate worship is as out of place as etchings in a kitchen. What is needed is an appreciation of the *principles* of reformed worship, together with a simple outline of the ascending movements involved, which may either be left simple or be adorned with all that art can supply. It is to the discovery of such principles, and to the devising of such a scheme, that we must now set ourselves.

I.

But we must first clear the ground. We all know that in the matter of order we have come into hopeless confusion. In many of our churches, even now, nobody (with the possible exception of the minister, and he is a doubtful exception) knows what is going to happen next. It is true that most city churches have printed orders; but whether the next hymn is to express praise, or penitence, or the missionary spirit, is a secret hidden until the hymn-book be opened; and when it comes to prayer, the congregation wanders, as on uncharted seas, moving from thanksgiving to intercession, from adoration to confession, and back again and round about and up and down. The result is that we sing with the spirit, but not with the understanding; and that the "long prayer" has become a clear invitation to inattention.

And yet there be some that say, why have an order at all? For, say they, an order becomes a routine, and a routine is the parent of a rut. It is familiarity, they maintain, that breeds inattention; whereas the unexpected and the diversified are the sources of sustained interest. In their support, they cite the example of such men as Dr. Joseph Parker and Mr. Spurgeon. The former often followed his own, fancy in the matter of order, while the latter, in his advice to his students, explicitly told them to change the order at their will. Their modern pupils lend ready ears to such counsel. It is reported that a minister, not long ago, was perturbed by the routine of Holy Communion, and so, to give variety, he sometimes administered the bread first and sometimes the wine. Anything for a change! An instance such as that puts a fool's-cap on the whole tendency, but rather undeservedly; for there are certain types of service in which the unexpected plays an important part; and, in suggesting guiding principles, it is necessary to distinguish services of that sort.

Now, there are two classes of services: as ministers have for long acknowledged by attempting a different type of sermon in the evening. My plea is that the distinction should be marked also in the tone and order of worship. The two sorts may be called (1) Services of Worship and (2) Services of Mission. The former of these are a supreme task of the Church and are ends in themselves. The latter are means to an end—namely, the extension of the kingdom. In Services of Mission, we may aim at diversity as much as we please, within the bounds of decency. As to that I have nothing to say; each man must work out his own methods, with due regard to his own personality and the type of community in which he is working. But in the case of Services of Worship, the situation is altogether different. In them the congregation is engaged, as a unity, in an act which requires a common understanding of every movement. The purpose cannot be fulfilled unless every member knows what he is doing and why he is doing it: and all this is impossible without an order.

Moreover, an order is demanded by two complimentary facts: namely, the Diversity and Unity of every congregation. Each body of worshippers is diverse, because it contains individuals in every kind of religious mood. One man will chiefly desire to confess his sins, while the next man's heart will be a tumult of thanksgiving. All of these moods have to be met; and an order is essential to secure that they shall be met. Otherwise, the leader will impose his own mood on the people, a thing that happens every Sabbath Day. But no less important is the unity of a congregation. The Object of Worship is One; and there is a "man in men," that responds uniformly, in normal circumstances, to His presence. Moreover, in the movement of "the man in men" towards God, all the diverse needs of the congregation are met. Our task, then, is to discover that normal response, and then to express it in the sequence of our worship.

II.

Two principles immediately make themselves manifest, without which no worship can be adequate. We may call them the principles of Alternation and of Ascension. Each deserves a little separate study.

1. *The Principle of Alternation.*

When a man approaches God, he will remember on the one hand, that it is God that he is approaching, and, on the other, that it is he that is approaching God. Inevitably, he will tend to swing from the thought of the holiness of the Worshipped, to the unworthiness of the worshipper: from God's law, to his own need of help: from the knowledge of God's everlasting mercy, to the answering thankfulness of his own heart. He will move rhythmically between Vision and Response. His worship will become an exchange between perception and his reaction thereto. Receiving from God and giving to God will follow, wave-like, one upon the other.

At this point, I find myself in some disagreement with those who see in worship only a series of developing attitudes on the part of the worshipper. They begin with Vision, indeed, but then proceed through Humility to Vitality and thence to Illumination and Dedication. That is good and helpful, as far as it goes; but it seems to miss the point that each response of the soul is conditioned by a new perception of God. True worship begins and ends with Vision, just as Dante's upward flight of the soul began with the sight of the Hill of Cleansing and ended with the flash of the unveiling of the Divine Reality. And as it thus begins and ends, so worship develops with new unfoldings of the Divine character, which call forth new answers from men, who, all the while, are drawing nearer to God, and, thus, discovering more clearly the Heavenly Father's face. Each Vision and Response is connected both with that which goes before and that which comes after; but they have a special relation to each other. A rightly ordered service thus consists in a sequence of pairs, consisting of a thought of God and the answer thereto, until we reach the final unveiling of the God of Grace and love and communion, in remembrance of whom we leave His house, to take up confidently our daily tasks.

2. *The principle of Ascension.*

In any considered approach to God, various emotions, it is clear, are developed in a normal mind. But it is not so generally recognized that, ordinarily, these are developed in an ascending scale. If we take the religious movement of the race as a whole, as it is displayed in the Bible, we can perceive an ascension from fear to awe, from awe to joy, and from joy to love. Our own experience corroborates this. The fear of the Lord is the *beginning* of wisdom: and the end of the story is to know and to rest in the love that passeth knowledge. And, midway, fear blends with awe: and awe at God's majesty moves into awe at His redeeming passion, whence springs joy that to ourselves is given new power and new life. From this we discover our key to the problem as to how worship must psychologically proceed. Beginning with an attempt to see the Vision of God high and lifted up, we progress along an inevitable movement of consequent fear blending into awe, and thence to a new unveiling of the Divine nature, whence spring joy and love. Once a minister has this sequence of mood clearly in his mind, the ordered ascent of his prayers will be secure; and there will be no more of the uncharted seas. He has discovered a guiding principle that will not fail him; for it is implanted in human nature, and, therefore, in his own.

But the ascent is not steady. As each new vision of God is perceived, there are often backwashes of feeling. This is especially true in the initial stages of worship, where we are thinking of God's holiness and of our inability to meet His demands. This backward swing must, I think, find expression in our order, as will hereafter be indicated. But the main movement is upwards, until we are lost in wonder, love and praise.

I daresay you have seen those clever gymnasts, who, beginning on a low-set trapeze, by a swing forward and backward gain momentum to catch a trapeze higher up, and so gradually ascend from bar to bar, until they reach the highest set before them. It is a crude image; but it may serve. In the main, our progress is simply upward in worship: but we require the backward movement to pass from fear and awe to joy. The depth of our need, and the depth of the waters crossed to satisfy it, must be realized before we can worthily praise the Deliverer. And all this a leader in worship will have in his mind as he sets himself to his task.

III.

Now that we have cleared the ground, and laid down these general principles, it is possible to deal with those practical problems, which are our chief concern. Let me ask you to imagine a body of normal people met together on a Sunday morning in an average church for the main act of weekly worship. Conceive them dropping in by twos and threes until eleven o'clock strikes, and the duty of the day has to be begun. What has to be done first? The answer is easy: we must draw near to God. We are not ready to worship yet. We have to "go unto the altars of the Lord." Our bodies may be in church, but our minds have to be brought and kept there, too. Wherefore, we set down first this highly important matter of

The Approach.

This consists of three steps: first, the call to attention; second, the attempt, in common, to realize the presence of God; and, third, the request for Divine aid in the enterprise on which we are about to engage.

Now, all this is of real importance. "Well begun is half-done." It is the first step that goes far to determine all the rest; and a minister should put forth a good deal of effort to create stillness and a sense of the Unseen *at the beginning.* Before the service opens, the average worshipper is anything but concentrated on the matter in hand. We are all human, and thoughts naturally wander about the church, noting latecomers, suspecting absentees and appraising new attire. God forgives it all, no doubt, for it is He that hath made us, and He remembers that we are dust. But it makes it the more important that certain preliminary steps should be taken to unify the congregation upon the duty before them. So first there comes—

(a) *The Call to Worship,* which takes the place of the "bell" in the Roman services. It may take the simplest of forms: indeed, the words "Let us worship God," said by a man who is listening to them himself, are all that is needed. But we must give them their full value as we say them. Let them (or whatever other words we use) be preceded by a slight pause, after we stand up. Our object is to *still* our people; and silence on our part is often the most effective way to do it. And as we utter the call, let us make an honest effort to hear it ourselves. We shall, thereby, communicate the stillness which our own hearts feel.

And what follows, inevitably, upon the call to attend? Why, clearly, a concerted attempt to secure, in common—

(b) *The Realization of the Presence of God.* Silence again is helpful, followed by such words as these, said or sung together—"Holy, holy, holy is the Lord of Hosts, the whole earth is full of His glory." It is difficult to find words more suitable than those of the Sanctus in Isaiah VI to express the united sense of God's majesty, which a congregation ought to endeavour to feel as they approach Him. Unfortunately, this sometimes is used in historic liturgy at quite a different part of the service; and we ought to follow historic usage, when we can. But the authority of Isaiah for the use of these words, as the expression of our first Vision of God, may justify us in departing from the later, though venerable, practice. However, we must find words of some kind, which can be used in common by the people, to express a thought of Him to whom they are approaching, which will stir in them that sense of right fear and awe, which is the beginning of wisdom in worship as in everything else.

Assuming, then, that the people's attention is rightly directed and that they are, severally, reminding themselves of the separateness of the object of their worship, what happens next? The answer suggests itself. They must ask God, without whose help no man can even approach Him, to aid them in their service. This they do in—

(c) *The Prayer of Invocation,* which is a call to God for aid in a particular enterprise—namely, the enterprise of that morning's worship. Too much care cannot be given to that prayer. A minister who does not know exactly how he is going to phrase it, before he goes into the pulpit, is seriously amiss. It should be short, cast in the collect-form, and should concern itself solely with the matter in hand. A perfect example is the opening collect of the Anglican Communion Office—"O, Thou before whom all hearts are open": and a man, who finds the composition of prayers especially difficult, might do worse than use this so expressive and so apt invocation of God's help every Sunday. Its delivery should never be hurried; each phrase should be quietly emphasized; so that all the worshippers may be touched with a sense of the magnitude of their request, as they appeal to God to cleanse the thoughts of their hearts that they may worthily magnify His holy Name.

With these three steps taken, the Approach is ended. We have gone unto the Altars of the Lord. We are ready now to enter on the morning's noble task, which henceforth must proceed upon the natural ascending alternations of Vision and Response. You observe that the alternation has already displayed itself. The thought of God has sent us asking help to worship. We shall find that a similar interchange will compel itself into our service to the end.

IV.

The Act of Worship.

A good image of our attitude as we enter on our enterprise is that suggested in the most familiar of the songs of Ascent. We lift up our eyes unto the hills in—

(a) *The Opening Adoration.* This is rightly
and properly sung by the congregation together.
We have to discover some hymn, which will con-
nect itself with the Approach and will conclude
with a statement of some aspect of the majesty
of God, in which we can worthily adore Him.
There is none better than that "grand old Puritan anthem," the 100th Psalm, set to Léon Bour-
geois' noble tune.   It carries on from what has
gone before, with its call to the whole earth to
"sing to the Lord with cheerful voice"; and it
ends with the Vision splendid of Him whose
"truth at all times firmly stood and shall from
age to age endure."   Those who are in perplexity
to find hymns which precisely fit into the various
parts of the service—and it is a sore business
to light on exactly what we want—might do a
deal worse than take a look at the Scottish
Metrical Psalms. They will find them peculiarly
rich in the noblest and simplest forms of opening
Adoration.

This done, there can be no question what we
must do next. The effect of the first unveiling
of God has been the same on humanity from the
beginning: and it will be the same until that
end comes, when sin shall be no more.   The

knowledge, that the Lord our God is righteous altogether, forces into our minds that related painful knowledge, that our thoughts are not His thoughts nor our ways His ways. Wherefore, our own nature compels us immediately to—

(b) *The Prayer of Confession, and for Pardon and Peace,* about which we need say little, except that it should be brief and as intimate, definite and sincere as we can make it—never forgetting, of course, that we are praying in public and on behalf of a congregation. Parts of the 51st Psalm will give us a model.

There may, however, be some difference of opinion as to what should follow. Many of our teachers send us at once to the regions of God's loving-kindness, whence He sends His healing and His strength. But I cannot think that the matter is quite as simple as all that. God does not let us off just because we say we are sorry; and He never, in any circumstances, ceases to demand obedience to His moral law. That surely ought to be expressed in every service. The weakness of some modern worship lies precisely here—that we have failed to make manifest austerity and sternness, as if the godly life were roses, roses all the way. Calvin knew better,

when he began every service with the recitation
of the ten commandments. Somewhere in the
order there ought to be given a glimpse of the
high and lofty places of that Law, which Christ
came not to destroy but to fulfil. And, if it comes
in naturally anywhere, it comes in at the point
we have now reached. It is true to experience,
that the first response of the Divine to the penitent is a renewed demand for obedience. A sense
that we must never desert from the paths of
righteousness comes over the mind, when earliest
we turn to God; and we realize that, whatever
God may be going to do as a result of our cry for
mercy, He is not going to change His mind about
godliness. This we may term—

(c) *The First Divine Response,* which will
consist in a short reading (or singing) of
some passage of Scripture, which sets forth the
moral responsibilities which God insists we shall
shoulder. The usual plan would, of course, be
to recite the ten commandments: but these basal
statutes of the embryo Hebrew state do not
"strike to within," on the modern mind. I think
it better to vary the passages here, using Deut.
VI:1-9 as the norm. But, whatever we may do
in the selection of passages, we must not fail to

bring in some clear expression of the moral law. Otherwise, we shall be true neither to the human nature we are expressing, nor to the God whom we are worshipping.

And what next? Again, we have only to ask our own hearts. What do we do, when conscience is hammering at us—when the stern Voice within is calling? We go down on our knees and tell God that, if obedience is to be forthcoming, He must help. Instinctively there follows—

(d) *The Prayer for Aid.* Very likely, we shall find it best to use a hymn or anthem for this. I am not concerned with the mode in which we work out the details: I am anxious only about the framework. And, at this point, a very human cry for the gift of the Divine strength must come in, or our worship will again be untrue to our need.

And then, what? Why, the Christian Evangel tells us. We have not only said that we are sorry, but we have faced the fact of conscience and have consequently flung ourselves on God: and the Bible was written and Christ lived and died that we may believe that God hears that

cry and answers it.   Wherefore, put down at
once—

(e) *The Second Divine Response:* which also
should consist of a passage or passages from
Scripture, telling of the Divine Compassion; of
the Love that will not let go; of the "how much
more" of God.

'Now, this opens a vexed and difficult question.
You observe that we have at most two readings
from Scripture, and that each is prescribed as
to subject.   That implies that large portions of
the Bible will never be read at the main occasion
of worship; and that the old idea of a lectionary,
which gradually takes us through the whole of
the Scriptures, will be set on one side.   I know
that many people gain their only knowledge of
the Word through reading from the pulpit—
more's the pity.   But that, surely, is only a reason
for securing that the passages read shall be of
the highest religious value.   The Anglican service, so beautiful with all its shortcomings, is
often hopelessly jarred by a couple of long,
irrelevant lessons from the two Testaments.
People who worship are hungry sheep, and
should be fed from the Word of God.   It seems
a pity to offer them David's pebbles from the

brook, or the measurements of the Tabernacle,
in place of bread. Consequently, some of us
will be of the opinion, that, in order to secure
the full emotive sequence of the service, a lectionary should be chosen which will confine itself, first, to the expression of the demands of
righteousness, and second, to a statement of the
Everlasting Mercy of Him who makes with us
a Covenant of Aid. And, if any one objects
that he wants to read a passage suitable to his
sermon, I reply that he can do that immediately
before he gives out his text, if he has a mind to:
and, further, that if passages setting forth God's
love in redemption are not relevant to his preaching, he had better take a thought and mend.

So here, in a passage taken from the N.T. (or,
better, in short passages from both Testaments),
we are given a Vision of the God of grace, "visibly in the world at war with sin." Whence, by
natural alternation, we proceed to—

(f) *The Related Responses of Thanksgiving
and Intercession.* The former of these may be
given in prayer-form or in song, or in both. It
may be expressed by the people together, or by
the choir. But let it be thanksgiving: and let

it be emphatic—for we have a multitude of benefits for which to give thanks to our Father.

And here, let me digress into a protesting question. Who started this trick of *beginning* services with the Doxology? Was he an Irishman,
with the entertaining gift, possessed by his race,
for inversion? It is quite obviously and startlingly wrong, if the progress of an order of worship is to be psychologically true. The right
place for a Doxology (or, better, the Te Deum)
is after the second Divine Response. We may
suppose the reason for its introduction was the
semi-laudable desire to "brighten" services: but
I confess that I never see prosperous citizens
fling back their shoulders, and, full-throatedly,
praising God from whom all blessings flow, at
the moment when they ought to be trying to be
still and know that He is God, without feeling
that I have strayed into a Rotary or Kiwanis
convention instead of into a church. No doubt
the practice will be difficult to stop: but one can
at least deliver one's soul by protesting.

Following upon the Act of Thanksgiving,
there naturally comes the Act of Intercession;
unless, indeed, some form of Creed is used. If
so, this is the place to recite it. The difficulty is

to find a form of words at once historical and expressive of sincere, modern belief. If the Church is to declare its faith, it must be the faith of the living Church that is declared. A simple Creed, in the language of Scripture, would be a great gain, if we could all agree on it. Meantime, most of us will tend to move straight on to the Act of Intercession, which follows so reasonably on Thanksgiving. We have been shown our Heavenly Father listening to our cry and, like children, we want to tell Him all about it—especially, about the hidden desires of our hearts for those we love. And we have been reminding ourselves of all the good things we have received, and, surely, like Christian folk, we want others to share in them, too. So, we intercede.

Now this is the high-water mark of endeavour in our worship. It takes the place of the Sacrament in the ordinary service: for, in part, it is sacrificial. When we intercede, on the one hand we ask from God what we desire to obtain for others, but have no means of securing, apart from God: on the other hand, we offer ourselves, implicitly, as agents, by whom the benefits for which we plead may be granted. This is, manifestly, a high and serious business: and the congregation must be keyed up to it. For this is the moment of Dedication. Intercession is a poor half-thing, if we do not desire the objects, which we are asking at God's hands, sufficiently to be able to say, whole-heartedly, that we are willing to be used by God for their accomplishment. If reality in worship is to be secured, the people must be alive and purposeful at this point: and the minister will give great pains to keep attention and to create an atmosphere of urgency during this prayer. It is rather humbling that it is notorious that the Intercession has often been the most wearisome part of the service. The next chapter will deal with the minister's task as a leader in prayer: but here it is sufficient to say that, whatever else he prepares for, he must prepare for the act in which he and his people put themselves in God's hand as His servants.

When the Intercession is ended, I like to sum up all our prayers in the prayer of our Lord. I think it comes best as a climax, and, unquestionably, it should be used at every service. But, never gabble it, as some so painfully do. Deliberately restrain the pace of utterance, in order that each clause may be duly alive in the mind. And, it is not a bad thing to have it printed in

front of you, where you can see it. Memory
plays strange tricks with us in the pulpit—especially with familiar words. I have thrice, in
public, stuck completely in this prayer: and the
memory of that discomfort makes me always
read it. And, then, when all has been gathered
up in Christ's own words, it is seemly to follow
with—

(g) *The Symbol of Dedication,* in the Offer-
tory, and some worthy word of Consecration and
renewed offer of service—a word in which it
would be well if the people could join. If they
do not, there is something to be said for always
using the same form of words, which the people,
knowing, can readily follow and adopt.

v.

Now, at this point, if we choose, we may lift
the congregation to the height of the Benediction,
and the morning worship will be complete. We
have moved from Preparation to Vision, from
Vision to Humility: from Humility we have
gained a new, austere Vision which has deepened
Humility; thence we have risen to the Vision
gracious, which, giving Illumination, spells Vital-

ity; and, then, after consequent Thanksgiving, we have dedicated ourselves to that God, whom we finally see as the changeless God of all grace in the Benediction. Our worship, if we choose, is complete.

But Protestantism believes in the vital importance of the illumination of the mind. Wherefore, we round off the service with a particular unveiling of God and His will through a human personality—that is, with a Sermon. The minister ceases to be "the man-in-men"; he turns from being the representative of the people to become a teacher and, possibly, a prophet. In order to let the mind move easily from the dominant acts of thanksgiving and intercession, he asks the congregation to sing a hymn appropriate to his sermon. He then preaches—always remembering that he and his people are still worshipping God. A quiet dismission hymn is, I think, desirable to let down attention before the people go into the street: but it should be short, simple and always familiar—a "grave, sweet melody." Then, with the ancient words of blessing—and let it be remembered that the benediction is a benediction and not a prayer—the eyes of the congregation are turned to the God of grace and

love and communion; and, with that comforting
vision before us, we turn again to the daily ways
of life.

Now, this puts the sermon where it belongs.
It has a place, a great place and a place all its
own, in the scheme of worship: but it is a sup-
plementary place. It gives an opportunity for
"particularizing" Vision; and therefore it is an
act of great dignity. But it is not the crown
of worship: and the other parts of the service are
not "preliminaries." Protestantism did a great
service when it reëxalted preaching: but it went
off the rails when it did so at the expense of
praise and prayer. Preaching will not lose, but
gain, when it is seen in proper proportion, and
when it is rightly related to other acts, in which
worship obtains a more complete expression.

VI.

The Practical Application of the Order.

Such, then, in outline is our scheme—the
frame-work into which we have to fit the details
of service. None of us will deny that the practical difficulties of adhering to a psychological
sequence are serious. Apart from finding suit-

able hymns and readings, what are we to do with Announcements, and Children's Addresses, and Anthems and Solos and Responsive Readings, and all the little diversities, with which we endeavour, usually dismally, to "brighten" the service?

As to Announcements we are all agreed: they are a public nuisance. Cut them down, if you cannot cut them out. Print them, if possible, and tell the congregation to read them. If that is too expensive, let them come after the worship-series is complete, just before the hymn before the sermon. In any case, decline to allow your pulpit to be made the free advertising-agency for all the events of the parish. Only announce churchly doings. And, above all, please do not be funny. Perhaps some psychologist can explain why the giving out of announcements in church is such a temptation to alleged humourists. Not, indeed, that humour is out of place in preaching, as we shall see later on, from the greatest of all examples. But the kind of witticisms to which the intimations tempt us are, as Dr. Johnson called the merriment of parsons, "mighty offensive." It is best to be on the safe side, and delete them altogether.

Children's Addresses, also, are on the whole, best omitted. It is true that people like them; but that does not prove a great deal. It is human to like candy. As a rule, these addresses affect the atmosphere and break the continuity. If the children are to be directly addressed, let the remarks to them be woven into the main sermon. For the rest, let the young children go out, and be looked after suitably by skilled women. And let the older ones sit still, and learn, by suffering, in their youth.

The "diversifyings" of the service can be left to each man's individual taste; always provided that they fit into the general scheme which we have been considering. Liturgical and responsive forms of prayer or praise can, obviously, be easily used. So can responsive readings, though, I confess, I question their worship-value. When their curious mumble comes up from the congregation, it is as if the clock had been put back, and grown folk were little boys and girls at Sunday School again. After all, the Psalms were meant to be sung, and not read, antiphonally. If we can rise to antiphonal singing, well and good. However, there is no law against a man adopting any method which keeps the attention of the congregation on the business in hand; but, every device must be estimated by its value for worship, and no diversity must be permitted which intrudes on the psychological order. Many of the "items" and "numbers" intended to brighten, sin dreadfully against that canon. They are, all too frequently, meaningless interjections suitable enough at an entertainment, but hopelessly out of place in church. After all, a church service is not an entertainment: it is an act of worship. The distinction is simple: and may reasonably be observed.

There remains the question of our music—a much more difficult matter. The mere choosing of hymns is a delicate task. We have to remember the point in the service at which a hymn is to come; the festival, it may be, of the Church year, which falls on the Sunday for which we are preparing; the diverse tastes of our musical high-brows and musical low-brows; and we must not forget old-time associations of particular words and tunes. No wonder so many ministers are prematurely bald. Above all, you have to remember your organist and choir. An ingenious commentator has suggested that St. Paul's thorn in the flesh was the music committee at

Corinth. Musicians, perhaps because they use that thought-medium which is supposed to be the language of heaven, are occasionally a little unearthly here below. Sometimes, one feels that Providence has compensated them for their noble gifts by denying them a whole share of common-sense. At any rate, a young minister will be very lucky if he does not find, sometime in the course of his career, that his church music affords him personal, as well as liturgical problems. This, at least, we all need to remember—that choirs are part of a congregation set to lead in a particular effort of worship, and not a separate guild with rights and privileges of their own. The ideal will be reached, when the whole con-gregation takes enough trouble about the music to become its own choir,—a consummation de-voutly wished, I am sure, by all musicians.

As things are, however, we must do with things as things will do with us; and our choirs are not only necessary, but are, normally, very helpful aids to worship. Some simple rules can be laid down, within whose bounds choirs should work.

They should, for instance, sit as in a church and not as if at a concert. The half-moon ar-rangement in front of the pulpit, to which many of us are condemned, is the worst conceivable. It is bad for the music, and distracting to the attention both of choir and congregation. The proper place for them is a chancel or the back gallery.

They should not attempt music beyond their range. That is a pearl of wisdom, if you like. But people, apparently, dislike acting on the over-obvious.

And their music should be *churchly*. Some of the solos sung in church only save themselves from being infuriating by being so comic. Those of us who are saved from this trial have much to be thankful for. On the other hand, good anthems and solos sung in sympathetic voices by singers who are themselves religious, have a worship value of the highest degree. They can take the place of prayers—very many of our hymns are suitable for that, too—if they are properly placed in the order of service. If co-operation is secured between the minister and the musicians—and it is usually easily enough obtained—and if there is mutual understanding as to the progression of the service, the choir part can be of the first importance in creating atmosphere.

But responsibility in the matter of music does not end with the choir. It lies at least as heavily on the congregation. There are two kindnesses which we may reasonably ask from our people in this region. First, those who cannot sing, should not. Congregational singing should not only be congregational, but singing. There are many amongst us whom the Lord evidently meant to sing with the spirit and with the understanding also; and to leave it at that. A man with a voice that has been treated with a fretsaw may want to sing: but, in common Christian charity, he should restrain himself. And, second, a congregation should educate itself in taste in psalmody and endeavour to get away from our distressing hymn traditions. It was Luther, I am told, who first said that the Devil should not have an exclusive right to the best hymn tunes: and it was Mr. Spurgeon who more recently gave voice to that opinion. It is a pity that these eminent men gave expression to such foolishness. The truth is, of course, that the Devil never had, nor can have, any of the best tunes. He jazzes and syncopates and is melodiously saccharine: but he hates the best tunes, and, knowing their influence for good, he tries to put the man in the street up against them by calling them "high-brow." An organist who stands up against all that type of opinion deserves respect: for he is standing for that beauty which is truth. And congregations—to say nothing of ministers—will endeavour to learn, from the men who know, how much deeper worship may be when the hymns have the dignity of plain-song, the strength of old chorales, and the rich nobility of the psalm tunes our fathers loved.

Well, these are practical matters, which young ministers must work out for themselves—with this comfort, that the reverent development of public worship is a man's job. If any one can say that he has helped to make more worthy the services of the Sanctuary, he can say that he is one of the company of God's workers, who have made two blades of grass appear where one grew before. The work demands patience, no doubt: but the result will crown the task.

VII.

Sometimes an example is more helpful than many precepts. Wherefore, I venture to append

an order of service, with the details filled in,
which is arranged upon the principles we have
been considering. It is, you observe, of the
simplest sort. We can, none of us, deny the
beauty of more elaborate services: but, on the
whole, we shall not err if we seek simplicity to
a greater degree than is now common. For
simplicity and nobility are born friends. In any
case, simplicity is no foe of the psychological
order, as you will see if you glance at the
following.

ORDER OF SERVICE.

I. *The Approach (or Preface)*

1. The Call — MINISTER. O come let us worship and bow down, let us kneel before the Lord our Maker: for He is our God.

2. The Realization — PEOPLE. Holy, holy, holy is the Lord of hosts, the whole earth is full of His glory:

3. The Cry for Help — MINISTER. Almighty God, unto whom all hearts be open, all desires known, and from whom no secrets are hid: cleanse the thoughts of our hearts by the inspiration of the Holy Spirit, that we may perfectly love Thee, and worthily magnify Thy Holy Name; through Christ our Lord. Amen.

II. *The Worship*
1. Vision
   &
   Humility
— *Psalm.* All people that on earth do dwell.
Prayer of Confession, and for Pardon and for Cleansing.

2. Vision & Deepened Humility	The Law. Deut. 6:1-9. The Anthem. Incline Thine ear . . .
3. Vision bringing Vitality and Illumination & Thanksgiving, Intercession & Dedication	The Lesson. Romans 8:31-39. Hymn of Thanksgiving, All Hail the Power of Jesus' name . . . Prayer of Thanksgiving, Inter- cession and Lord's Prayer. Offertory. MINISTER. Receive these sym- bols of Thy people's labour, Lord, and be pleased to use alike them and us for the Kingdom of Thy Son, for His Name's sake. (Announcements, if any.)
4. The Particular Vision & Illumination	Hymn. Oh Master let me walk with Thee. Sermon. Psalm 23:3. (Brief Prayer.) Hymn. The King of Love my Shepherd is.
5. The Final Vision & Gift of God.	The Benediction.

You see how that service swings in alternation, and how it ascends until at last we stand before the God who blesses us—the God of the Everlasting mercy, who calls us into communion with Himself, giving us that universal grace, which is His changeless gift to His children. If we and our people can reach thither for a moment, and find our hearts softened and comforted, we may know the labour of our worship has not been in vain in the Lord.

CHAPTER II.

NO part of public worship is easy work for the minister; but the most testing of all is leadership in prayer. For, then, he becomes the "man-in-men," at once self-forgetful and self-mindful: forgetful of his mood, however dominating it may be; and mindful of his unchanging needs as a sinful man. In prayer, the congregation is at the human end of the "swing" of worship. Prayer, in public worship, is the action of response to the Vision of God—and thus it displays man both at his puniest and his greatest. The whole of the ascending scale of religious reaction has to be expressed. No wonder that a man, who takes his work seriously, hesitates and is afraid before entering on such a task, and is thankful, if, without a too painful poverty of feeling and word, he comes to a conclusion. And still less wonder that so large a section of the Church has turned to liturgy, whereby each minister becomes the mouthpiece of the devout mind of the whole Church. After all, nothing can be better than the best; and if men, who were greatly gifted in language and sensitive in heart, have left behind them the words in which they gave form to humanity's religious need, why should not lesser men thankfully use them, and thus defend their congregations from the poor inadequacy of their own devotional speech and understanding?

And yet no Reformed Liturgy is wholly satisfactory—not even the English Prayer Book, which is the common possession of us all and so peculiarly dear to those who have been brought up in its use. For, as we all know, its Morning Prayer (with which alone we are here concerned) is a combination of ancient offices, and the patchwork shows. It has its roots in the ordered services of the monasteries, and, therefore, assumes that the main worship-occasion of the day—the celebration of the Sacrament—is over or is still to come. And, apart from such considerations, there are flaws in it, if we take as our test its psychological development. The opening, for instance, is far too abrupt. We are not prepared to be flung so quickly into confession; and, to my mind, absolution follows too easily and too quickly. While none of us can pay too much respect to this noble manual of devotion, we can still hold that the Universal Reformed Liturgy has not yet been discovered. There is work still to be done. It would be a strange instance of Time's revenges, if the descendants of the Puritan and the Covenanter should hand back to their brethren of the Anglican tradition a liturgy on which all could unite. Stranger things have happened, if the interest displayed in America about orders of service contains within it anything of a prophecy. But one thing is sure—the ultimate liturgy will not be wholly liturgical; for no liturgy *can* be complete. Leading in prayer is unquestionably aided by personality—as we all shall agree, who can remember occasions, when some true man of God raised the prayer-mood of a congregation by his own close contact with the Unseen. There must always be an opportunity for free prayer, to be used by those who can use it: and the Churches of our lineage, in retaining the spontaneous expression of our common needs have been retaining something of real worship-value.

But this only makes our mishandling of ex-

58 PUBLIC WORSHIP OF GOD

tempore prayer the more distressing. For we
have mishandled it dreadfully, and still do. Our
lack of sequence, our neglect of necessary elements, our startlingly unsuitable language are
manifest on every hand. No doubt, they are, in
part, due to a reaction from formalism; but they
also spring from a thoroughly unreal dependence
upon the guidance of the Spirit, and from plain
thoughtlessness and lack of preparation. As a
result, we hear the prayers that we do hear—
prayers theological, prayers oratorical, prayers
bright and brotherly, (as, "O Lord, give us
pep"),—prayers of any and every sort, except
devotional. "Paradoxical as it may appear unto
Thee, O Lord," is the alleged beginning of a
prayer by an argumentative, metaphysical Scot.
If anything does appear paradoxical to the perfect Mind, it is the granting of the title "prayer"
to some of the disquisitions which we submit in
worship. It is no wonder at all that men sigh,
not so much for the beauty, as for the safety
of a liturgy.

I.

And yet the reasons for retaining free prayer
are obvious and conclusive. Its proposed per-

mission, in the present revision of the Prayer Book, shows that its desirability is apparent not only to Puritans: and the fact that our people hold to it so tenaciously indicates that they have found in it qualities of value. As we have already indicated, it affords opportunity for a sensitive mind to awaken the prayer-mood in other minds: and, even if a minister be a very ordinary person, as is normally the case, yet his friendship for his people and their friendship for him, will lend power to the inflection of his voice, and to his turns of phrase, to create the devotional atmosphere in which true prayer can speed upon its way.

But, more generally, free prayer must continue to be used because of its elasticity. It surely is not true that the language which is most helpful to one type of congregation is most helpful to all types. In spiritual needs men may be much of muchness ("there is no difference" the Apostle emphatically declares); but intellectually there are clearly disparities. Language which is archaic has an added dignity to ears attuned to English; but it is only unreal to simpler folk. And an elasticity, which will make the content of our intercessions native to our own

time, is an unchallengeable good. The touch of
conscious superiority, for instance, in a prayer for
"Jews, Turks and Infidels" is not genuine from
the lips of men of today. It is with quite a different accent that we can pray, sincerely, for the
spreading of the kingdom. And inasmuch as
all prayer must be free from the mere suspicion
of unreality, stereotyped forms have to be continually reädjusted, especially in intercession.

This leads, naturally, to one of the main de-
fences of non-liturgical forms. We need elasticity in order that we may be *particular*. It is
this want, doubtless, that has caused permission
for free prayer to be suggested in the Prayer
Book. Definiteness—particularity, if you prefer
it—is desirable in confession, in supplication and,
frequently, in thanksgiving: but it is the root of
the matter in intercession. We must not forget
to pray for "all sorts and conditions of men";
but we are not going to create a great eagerness
of pleading in a congregation, unless we pray
for the particular sort and condition which that
congregation has in its heart. Take the case of
a fishing-village on a stormy Sunday; or a min-
ing-town, when there has been an accident; or
an industrial centre, when there is a strike or a

lock-out,—it is inhuman not to pray specifically
for those immediately affected. Those present
are thinking of nothing else. They want to tell
God all about it—and where are they to do that
better than in His house? Even if the whole
community is not affected, why should not individuals in special need be given to feel that the
Christian Body is praying with them? A mother
has bad news from abroad: or her son is a sailor,
and his ship is overdue: mental trouble has
touched, maybe, her first-born. Her minister
knows about it—why should he not have opportunity to pray for those, in lands afar, whose
names are graven on our hearts; or for those
whose ways are in the great deep, that the seas
may be still about them; or for any who have
lost the kindly light of reason? A form of
prayer, which makes such special intercession
impossible, is sending the Church out, crippled,
to one of its main tasks: and for that reason alone unrestricted prayer will be jealously
guarded by Churches which have known its
benefits.

One other reason for its retention may be alleged. If (and much emphasis has to be placed
on that word)—*if* a minister takes his leadership

in prayer with due seriousness, he has a new
incentive and aid to ministerial effectiveness.
For, if he is to be the mouthpiece of his people
in prayer, he must meditate alone by himself;
he must have the pastoral mind; he must dwell,
not only with the language, but with the thoughts
of devotion. His duties in prayer may be his
own chief education. It would not be a foolish
contention that the best qualities of the Puritan
minister have had their spring just here.

II.

If free prayer is to do what we claim for it,
certain conditions have to be observed. It *must*
be prepared for—both directly and indirectly.
We have to remember that worship is a task;
and that the Holy Spirit inspires through
thought. Moreover, preparation is demanded by
the fact that, seeing that the minister is the
mouthpiece of all the people, he has to express
all the normal emotions that will touch them as
the service proceeds. Not only so, but he must
express them as they arise, and, therefore, he
must never depart from the psychological order
—invocation, confession, prayer for pardon,

prayer for aid, thanksgiving, intercession and dedication. He must set aside his own moods with a firm hand—particularly if he be a man of a sorrowful spirit. He is not there to tell God, *via* the congregation, about his own megrims. And, above all, he will remember that indirect preparation is more important than direct. To be equipped to lead in prayer any Sunday is a better thing than to be prepared with prayers for next Sunday.

Students, and those who are young in the ministry, may not be averse to a little practical advice as to the preparation and as to the act of leadership itself in the Sanctuary. It must, of course, be remembered that this, like preaching, is an individual thing, and that methods of preparation which are one man's food may be another man's poison. Some general rules, however, may be laid down; and for the rest, practices, which have been tried by one man and found helpful, are at least worth the consideration of those who come after him.

(a) Public prayer is the pastoral office at its height. Therefore, a man must keep close to his people *religiously*. We shall be concerned later with pastoral work in relation to preaching; and

for the moment it is enough to observe, that a
man is only able to express people's needs, so
as to touch their hearts, if he knows them—and
that not in the casual, social way, but, as a minister should know them, in their hidden needs.
There are enormous practical difficulties, ob-
structing the pastoral office, in modern conditions; but it is possible, gradually to get our
people to visit us, if we have not time to go to
them.   If we succeed in developing a relation
with our flock, in which they will naturally come
to us, we may be sure that it is in their troubles
that they will come; whereby we gain, slowly,
that knowledge of the human heart, which is
lacking in those whose experience is inexperience.
In his first charge, however, a minister ought to
be able to visit his parish easily, and he should
use his visits so that a religious contact will be
established.   From the confidences so given, a
man will learn that which will make living and
actual, not only his intercessions, but all his
prayers—and, not least, his confessions.   And,
at all times, there is one object of pastoral care,
whom he should not, and need not, forget—to
wit, himself.   Let us take a good look at ourselves
in God's presence, and we shall not lack some

equipment for expressing the simple needs of our people.

(b) Secondly, we should plan our week, setting apart particular days, or portions of days, for particular tasks; and, in that plan, keep one morning for the arrangement of our service and for indirect preparation for prayer. If we start that practice when we are young, and in our first charge, when we are old we shall not depart from it.

Here let me pay a tribute to the memory of a great leader in prayer—the greatest I have ever known, who taught me long ago the rudiments of worship, not only by precept but by the wonder of his example—I mean the late Dr. Oswald Dykes. His power of raising the devotional tone of a service was unrivaled in my experience. He frequently read his prayers; but when he did not, his mind seemed such a storehouse of knowledge of the human heart and of language in which to convey it, that to be led in prayer by him was an experience not to be forgotten. Dr. Marcus Dodds—a man not given, one would think, to outbursts of enthusiasm—is alleged to have said that he had heard better preachers than Dr. Dykes, but that he would go across London to hear him pray. Unless students have changed since my time, they agree with the Psalmist that "it is vain to rise up early"; and with Mr. Gladstone that "getting up in the morning is the most disagreeable duty of the day." But, when I was at my theological college (although I was, and am, in whole-hearted agreement with Mr. Gladstone), I, in common with all the rest, rose with alacrity to be at early chapel, when Dr. Dykes was to take it. A man, surely, had remarkable powers who affected people so different as Dr. Dodds and us young men.

And how did he gain them? Well, he told me himself: by sheer, hard toil. One morning a week (Thursday, I think) was rigidly set apart for the preparation of prayers. Sometimes, he would make as many as forty attempts to get the precise thought and rhythm which he wanted for the prayer of Invocation. And, for the rest, he read, and went on reading, all the manuals of devotion of all the Church, until he walked in equal company with the great leaders in prayer of long ago.

That is, it is clear, a severe programme: and we shall not adopt it, unless we are eager to be truly effective in this department of our work. Few of us have had sufficient character to stick to it completely. But it is the right example. We should have on our desks the Prayer Book; every worthy modern service book we can find; the *Preces Privatae* of Bishop Lancelot Andrews should be within reach ("Lancelot Andrews, who taught most of us to pray," as Dr. Alexander Whyte used to say); and, above all, we should read, meditatively, over and over, the Psalms and the Prophets in King James' Version, so that devotional thought and devotional language will become part of the permanent furniture of our minds.

(c) We should commit to memory—especially collects and special prayers from the Prayer Book and large portions of the devotional passages of the Bible. Not, indeed, to be able to quote them, for the spatch-cocking of learnt prayers or verses into our own free prayer usually gives an impression of disjointedness: but in order that our own language may be insensibly fashioned thereby.

(d) As we read and commit to memory, we should attune our ears to rhythm. For it is only through rhythmical language that the nobler ideas can be hinted. "Language is given us" as the French cynically say, "to conceal our thought"—and even if that is not true, the kind of idea with which we are concerned in prayer easily breaks through our poor language and escapes. But, by means of rhythm, we can suggest to the mind something of the greatness which lies beyond our thought. To say "God is great" is to say something true: but the expression lies on the surface of the mind. It touches no deep spring of feeling. But if a man speaks of God as "Thou who coverest Thyself with light as with a garment," or as One "whose dwelling is the light of setting suns"; or who "inhabiteth eternity, whose Name is holy," the "beat" of such phrases, as well as their imagery, helps to express something of the sense of the Divine Majesty. And it is only by study and by storing the memory, that a man will naturally fall into the right kind of rhythm of the right kind of words, when he leads his people in prayer.

(e) During the first five years, at least, of his ministry, a man should write out his prayers. Whether he reads them or not in the pulpit is his concern: but he assuredly should write until he has at his disposal a set for every Sunday in the year, both morning and evening—a hundred and four sets in all. Even if he never uses them, the effect on his powers of extempore expression will be admirable. And, always, however long his experience may be, he should know by heart his prayer of Invocation—and have said it over and over before he goes into the pulpit: for so much depends on the reverence and the rightness of the opening.

III.

In conclusion, let a few general counsels be added.

(a) Take your people into your confidence about your order of service in general, and the sequence of the prayers in particular. Explain it to them from time to time. Let them know precisely what you are trying to do on their behalf. Only so, will they be able to follow intelligently.

(b) Announce, in suitable language, each main division of prayer—as thus:—"let us confess our sins unto Almighty God"; "let us beseech God for His pardon and cleansing"; "let us give thanks unto our Lord, who is good, whose mercy endureth forever." These, and like phrases, recall the attention of the congregation and concentrate it on the next effort. Before each of these announcements, and after them, let there be a slight pause—not too long, but quite perceptible. Occasional, brief stillnesses are markedly helpful to attention.

(c) Let the prayers be many and short, rather than few and long. The power of mental concentration in a congregation is limited—and a minister should not overstrain it. This is a matter particularly to be watched in the Intercessory Prayer, which is of necessity the longest, especially if it follows immediately after the prayer of thanksgiving. Break it up into related sections, e.g. the nation, the Church, the sorrowful, etc.: and pause slightly between the sections. Often use a form akin to that of a "bidding" prayer, in which little more is done than to recite a list of the classes for which we pray: and, again, have little pauses after each class is mentioned. Too steady a flow of speech in prayer can become dreadfully monotonous, and makes attention difficult. We can avoid that unfortunate result, by cultivating the little pauses. But they must not be exaggerated. There is only a certain amount of silence that worshippers can stand. Quite soon, it gets on people's nerves. Wherefore, if we use silence, we must be careful not to overdo it. Too much is worse than too little.

(d) Keep the voice as low as is consistent with being heard. All harshness and "edge" to the tone should be removed, as well as all uncontrolled shoutings. It is not in the least edifying to hear a man screaming at his Maker, in a kind of eldritch shriek, to "hear these our humble breathings." Avoid any appearance of orating: and, to this end, be very careful about both adverbs and adjectives. The best rule is to cut them both out, unless we are compelled (as when naming God, or describing His action) to put them in. A study of the collects in the Prayer Book will prove, perhaps to our surprise, how very economical they are in their use of these descriptive parts of speech.

(e) And, finally, while it is true that in prayer we are at the human end of the worship-swing, let us remember that in prayer we are addressing God. It is quite wonderful how the memory of that plain fact helps us to reach after thought which shall be sincere and language which shall be noble. If, along such lines as these, we do our best to cultivate our faculties, we may be surprised to find how content our people are, to be led in prayer after the simple fashion of our fathers.

CHAPTER III.

FIRST of all, I want to ask a plain question, to which I should like (but shall not get) a plain answer. Do you, in your heart of hearts, believe in preaching? There is a vast deal of it done every week, and nothing particular seems to happen to the world as a result. It is not in the least unreasonable to enquire, if, consequently, you really think that there is very much in it; or whether you do not believe that the honest men, who toil in its preparation and perspire in its delivery, would not be more fruitfully occupied in some other way.

Quite a lot of people, nowadays, would unite in disparagement. "Is he a good preacher?" a Scottish professor was asked. "Admirable," was the reply: "he does remarkably little harm." "Am I a D.D.?" indignantly queried an American scholar. "No, sir: I am not. Why, they give the wretched degree for *preaching.*" High

Churchmen are often frankly scornful: though not quite as scornful as certain high-brow students of my acquaintance in the old days, who regarded a popular preacher as almost certainly a charlatan. If preaching was to be permitted, their ideal setting for it was a dirty church in a back street, where a long-haired scholar discoursed on the Hexateuch to the intellectually elect. So, I quite seriously want to know—do you young ministers or students, who may read this, believe in the importance and the power of the spoken word? For my own part, I do so believe: and for the belief I see reasons and reasons.

(a) In the first place, it was the chief task of our Lord. It was His own way of advancing the kingdom. "He departed thence to teach and to preach in their cities," we read. And what was good enough for Him is surely good enough for us.

(b) Further, great periods in the history of the Church have been marked by great preaching. After Christianity had laid hold on the Empire under Constantine, and the Church began to spread widely, both East and West flung up men whose names as preachers stand high

in the roll of fame; for, in the East, Chrysostom
appeared and, in the West, Augustine. So
much, indeed, was preaching an agency for the
spread of Christianity, that Julian the Apostate
(when, after Constantine, he attempted to re-
store the pagan culture) organized preachers to
commend the old faith. An imitation of that
kind is not only the sincerest form of flattery,
but a proof of the power of the method imitated.
In the thirteenth century, after an arid period
in the Church's life, when Christian Europe felt
the sudden shock of the mighty personalities of
St. Dominic and St. Francis, and when learning
reawakened and, afar off, there might be heard
the beginning of the stirring notes of the Reformation, it was by preaching that the Dominicans
and the Franciscans—but particularly the former—carried their new energy amongst the
people. So great was the reputation of the
Dominican as a preacher, that it persists to this
day. I have seen an Italian village church,
amongst the hills, crammed to the doors on a
lovely spring afternoon to hear a Dominican
friar. And when the Reformation burst, in all
its storm and majesty, upon Europe, once more
preaching came into its own. Luther, Zwingli,

Calvin, Knox—these, indeed, were names to conjure with in pulpits, as in the council-rooms of kings. In England, when the commonwealth was divided by convictions, partly religious and partly political, so real that men were prepared to die for them, both the Cavaliers and the Puritans produced a race of preachers stronger, some would say, than any who have succeeded them. On the one hand, Hooker, Donne, Thomas Fuller and Jeremy Taylor: on the other, Cartwright, Richard Baxter, John Owen, John Bunyan, Thomas Goodwin—these formed a galaxy of power that is still our pride. Even a civilization such as that of Louis XIV, because it was a great civilization tinctured with Christianity, produced pulpit artists. Bossuet, Bourdaloue, Massillon and Fénélon attested at least the culture of that notable time. And, nearer our own day, when the mind of Scotland was flung into a ferment by the controversy that issued in the Disruption, and the Church was a living thing in men's thoughts, the leaders were preachers also. Chalmers and Candlish themselves would have said that the pulpit, rather than the Assembly platform, was their throne. When, in the brilliant, dead eighteenth century, the flame of religion in England was kept alive by Methodism, it was as a preacher that John Wesley went forth; and when, in the nineteenth century, there arose in the Church of England the movement toward Catholic practice which breeds such fruit today, it was the compelling voice of Newman in St. Mary's, Oxford, that gave it its impetus and direction. And who has ever heard of a revival that had no preaching-man in its centre? Your revival assumes your Moody. But we need not go so far afield for our evidence. The ordinary well-filled church in Britain, or Canada, or the States, has a man in its pulpit, who can preach decently. "A house-going ministry makes a church-going people," is one of those statements which have the colour of truth without the reality of it. If it means that you must know your people and preach to *them,* well and good. But if it means that you can chatter inanities from the pulpit, and still have your church full, provided you have knocked at a sufficient number of doors during the week, it is plain nonsense. Your people prefer to have your best out of your head rather than out of your heels. On the whole, we may agree that history and present experience alike are against the superior modern who sneers at the spoken word.

But I do not suppose that it is necessary to labour this point to the majority of those who may read this. We are already convinced, by that potent argument, personal experience. We know for ourselves the effect of "truth strained through a human personality," as a sermon may well be defined. For myself; I have been at great festivals of the Church in some of the stateliest fanes of Christendom—and they remain vague, if noble, memories. But, sharp and clear-cut in the storehouse of the mind, stand one or two occasions, when men, who for themselves had tasted and seen how gracious the Lord is, spoke of the love that had set them free. No one, who can remember any such occasion, can doubt· the possibilities of the preacher. Wherefore, let all ministers of our branches of the Church, hold to the old view, that this is their main job. To it they must give their steady application, refusing to be drawn aside by the multifarious, busy-idle distractions of this fussy age. A writer in an English paper, not long ago, wrote this comment on a promising divine:—"Mr. ——— is still well on the sunny side of forty, and if he resists the temptation to let himself be melted down for the tallow trade, in a day of movements and causes, he will make a distinctive contribution to the religious life of his generation." An admirable hint, this, for the young. Conference-itis is a devastating fever. It melts down for the tallow trade those that should be letting their light shine in that little corner, which is their own pulpit. The weekly instruction, as good as we can make it, is the proud tradition and contribution of our Church. Let us see to it that we give the best we have.

I.

At any rate, we are agreed that preaching is sufficiently important for us to enquire somewhat about it. And, first, let us be clear as to its *object*. What does preaching propose to do?

The answer is two-fold. Preaching intends, (1) to glorify God, and (2) to help men to be good. The latter of these is the *immediate,* and the former the *final,* object of the spoken word. Thus, preaching allies itself both with the Vision and with the Responsive Need, which we noticed to be inevitably linked in worship. It is intended

to give Illumination which shall bring Vitality—
to use technical language. In setting forth the
facts of God, it glorifies Him; in relating them
to mankind, it provides help for the needy.

Never let us forget this double significance of
our pulpit work: and always let them be expressed in terms as direct as these. Matters of
importance can usually be put in simple language. Certainly, this matter can. We prepare
in our studies, and we speak in our pulpits, in
order to show forth the glory of our Maker and
thus to help men, ourselves especially, to be good.
If we keep the former of these objects before us,
we go far to solving some of our problems; as
for instance, the problem of the permissible range
of subjects for preaching. We are put in pulpits
in order to glorify God: which, at any rate, keeps
certain types of absurdity and indecency out of
our churches.

II.

The immediate object of preaching is secured
in one of two ways, or by a blending of the two.

(a) By a presentation of *truth*. A text which
ought to be emblazoned in every minister's study
is "Ye shall know the truth and the truth shall

make you free." To make our faith credible: to convince the minds of our hearers that God and sin and love and the indwelling spirit are *facts*—here is the dignified enterprise on which we may embark Sunday by Sunday, knowing that, if we can succeed, the immediate object of preaching has been achieved. Once a man is convinced of a truth he is strengthened with might. And have we not sadly to admit that our modern preaching is weak here, compared with the standards of former days? No doubt, we have a harder task than our fathers, who could clinch a doubtful argument with a "proof-text." No doubt, knowledge has grown from more to more, and the modern, intelligent congregation cannot be put off with half-reasoning. But have we not shrunk from our task because it is hard, instead of regarding its difficulty as a challenge? The fact remains that the condition of sustained, effective preaching is wide knowledge and good, hard thinking: and that young ministers must scorn the sophistry that tells them that their congregations will not listen to theological sermons. The truth is the exact opposite—they will not listen long to anything else. Of course, the language must not be the technical language of the class-rooms of a by-gone age: but theology expressed in comprehensible speech is essential. After all, what is theology but considered commonsense applied to the meaning of life and the relations of God and man? Let us pay our congregations the very slight compliment of believing them to be rational beings who want to know, and who hold that "thought is the citadel." Unless we stiffen our preaching, and replace the iron of argument in it, the Reformed Church will die of pernicious anæmia.

(b) Secondly, the immediate object of preaching is achieved by *awaking the emotions*. This sounds the simpler method, and most men try it. Congregations are curiously sentimental; and sometimes seem to like to have their emotions stirred by fat fingers. The audiences that are attracted by praters, who pull out the *vox humana* stop at the beginning and keep it on all the time, are depressingly large. "Sob-stuff" is almost a synonym for much preaching today. But the degradation of emotive pulpit work must not blind us to its possible splendour. For preaching of this sort, at its height, is poetry. Here, preaching becomes an art, fit to rank with the noblest arts of them all. Imagination and feeling have to be blended with the glory of words in a delicate and sensitive mind. Nor is thought to be neglected; poems are thought transfused with feeling and conveyed through images portrayed rhythmically. He that proposes to preach in this way is set on a road that seeks the hill-tops.

A curious change is to be observed in this type of work in recent times. A generation ago, a sermon, designed to appeal to the emotions, would, three times out of four, have appealed to the emotion of fear: whereas, nowadays, you will search far before you find a minister using the "hangman's whip." "Hold them over the pit," is advice which, today, only brings a smile. Do you think that it is a justified smile? Do you find life so bereft of the stern and the tragic, that we can afford not to be frightened? Does God, in His strong mercy, never scare us? We shall do well to remember that He, at least, plays upon the whole of the ascending emotive scale of fear, awe, joy and love: and that preachers are not loyal to all they should have learned in experience, if they are never afraid themselves, and, consequently, compelled to communicate their fear to their hearers. However, it is doubtless best to touch mostly upon the strings at the upper end of the emotive scale, remembering "the expulsive power of a new affection"; and knowing that, though reason may fail to change a man, if you "touch the lever of his affections, you move his world."

III.

Before we proceed to practical advice upon the preparation of sermons, one further general consideration should be mentioned, which is of real importance in these days—namely, that, if preaching is to secure its immediate object of helping men to be good, the preacher must bear in mind that each man is an *individual:* to the individual the appeal must be made.

Now, this is fundamental, and requires to be said. Our subject may be the kingdom, and the general welfare of humanity: but our immediate object is to help, not humanity, but Brown, Jones and Robinson, sitting there in the pews in front of us, to be good. And these persons are intensely individual—solitary and separate. In the deepest of senses it is true that we mortal millions live alone; that "we stand upon isles, who stand." Indeed, we are strangers, not only to one another, but to ourselves. It is this that makes life so hard—that we walk as pilgrims chained to a self that is the unknown, and seems the unknowable. No man hath seen himself, at any time. "Know thyself" counseled the wise Greek. If only we could! But God has placed a boundary to our knowledge of ourselves, saying, thus far and no farther. Francis Thompson has given vivid expression to this inaccessibility of the soul in his poem "The Fallen Yew." He imagines a wife calling to her mate on her marriage-day, "I take you to my inmost heart, my true"; and then turns on her with the savage declaration that she does not possess the keys to the citadel of her personality and cannot yield them to any lover.

> "Ah, fool, but there is one heart you
> Shall never take him to.
>
> .　　.　　.
>
> "The hold that falls not when the town is got,
> The heart's heart, whose immured plot
> Hath keys yourself keep not!
>
> .　　.　　.
>
> "Its gates are deaf to Love, high summoner;
> Yea, Love's great warrant runs not there;
> You are your prisoner.
>
> .　　.　　.
>
> "Its keys are at the cincture hung of God."

When we are forced back on ourselves, the stark truth of a poem such as this bludgeons the mind. We dwell in mystery—the mystery of vastness, the mystery of Whither and of Whence. But we do not need to go to the ends of the earth to find the incomprehensible. Ourselves are mystery. The most untravelled country of all is the secret country of our own hearts.

What, then, about preaching and the preacher? His task is to appeal to the individual—to the Ever-hidden—in such a way that the spiritual levers of action may be touched—levers which are locked in the citadel. How can he set about a business such as that? Not at all, save he remember that the keys of the heart's heart "are at the cincture hung of God." It is only by letting loose divine forces that preaching can do its work—a reflection, surely, which gives a final dignity and solemnity to our duties. A preacher, in the end, is only a tool in a mightier Hand— or, at best, only the humble agent through which the transforming energy may flash, or by whom it may be set free. Let us never forget that, as we preach, we are dealing with forces over which we have no control, and that it is possible—let us be still and afraid before the possibility—to let them loose wrongly. The preacher who, for instance, carelessly plays upon the emotion of

fear, is a man who may have to answer terrible
questions some day. A boy with a match in a
powder magazine is wisdom and safety compared
with him. I am not likely to forget the strained,
scared eyes I once saw in a girl's pale face one
Sunday night, when, before a massed congregation, a minister was using all his powers of voice
and language and magnetism to frighten the
people: and, in so doing, was uttering falsehoods
about God and His dealings with men. I can feel
the tenseness of the hushed church, while the
wonderful voice from the pulpit, stilled to a
whisper, declared that not to have *felt* the love of
God was to be lost. Sheer falsehood; for feeling
is a *reward,* and many a time waits upon death
before it comes. But there was no question but
that power was let loose that night, and that one
poor girl was being scared away from her
Heavenly Father. And what was wrong with
that minister was that he was obviously not prepared. Such instances, we shall hope, are not
common. But the fact that, when we preach, we
are in touch with powers unseen is enough to
make us take this matter seriously. For, while
we have to avoid letting loose these energies
wrongly, our main purpose is to let them loose

rightly. "Christianity is a power, or it is nothing," and its preaching must unchain power or it is not preaching. The most severe criticism I have heard of our pulpit work today was given not long ago by a lady. "It's nearly all a knotless thread," she said. No grip, no catching-point in it. Much of it is clever; some of it—too much perhaps—is entertaining; a little of it is brilliant. But it can be all these and remain a knotless thread—a thing that slips through the mind, pleasantly it may be, like the sound of a very lovely voice, but ineffectively, leaving no trace. Let us watch our lists of young communicants, and of those who come to us in trouble, to see if our preaching is fastening and holding anywhere. For all our work is useless unless it grips—and in gripping, heals and strengthens the separate hearts and wills of those who hear us.

IV.

Of course, this emphasis upon the individual does not prevent us from preaching about the kingdom, but quite the contrary. For the individual will not reach his perfection apart from the whole. Readers of Dante (and all ministers and students should be that) will remember the lovely image of the perfected community which he portrays in the Rosa mystica—the white Rose of Paradise. There each petal is a separate soul, come to its full stature, and fair as only the petals of a rose can be. But, clearly, each possesses and retains all the rest, in the living flower. "They without us cannot be made perfect" is at once comforting and inspiring.

At the same time, let us never forget that, when we preach about communal good, it is to individuals that we are speaking. Jesus, it is true, came preaching the kingdom: but He chose twelve very individual individuals to whom He especially declared it. His point of attack was the individual conscience. So we, when we preach on social duties, must not vaguely shoot our arrows into the air, but must have the specific members of our congregation as our targets. If we do that, we are likely to be more effective for the cause we have at heart. Moreover, we shall do well to keep in mind the old, old wisdom that the changed society will come through changed men and women. The declaration of social righteousness is undoubtedly a duty of the Christian pulpit, but it is neither the whole, nor the

chief, duty. In any case, we have all to be as
sure as we can that the social schemes we pro-
pound are both righteous and reasonable. Before we talk too largely and emphatically about
social reconstruction, it is not unseemly to have
a knowledge of economics—a singularly re-
condite and difficult subject. Inasmuch as
hardly any of us possess the requisite knowledge,
it behooves us to speak with due modesty and
restraint. Meantime, we have the fundamental
religious principles of the Bible to declare; we
have Christ Himself to proclaim; and we need
not have any fear that men who take discipleship
to Him seriously will rest content with a system
which inflicts unnecessary injury or injustice on
the least of these His brethren. And, if ever we
feel that we are beating the air, and that all
our toil is futile, let us call to mind that, in all
this business we are "labourers together with
God." It is rather wonderful work about which
a thing like that can be said.

CHAPTER IV.

THE PREPARATION OF A SERMON.

THIS chapter is purely practical, and consists mainly of that which is alleged to be
the only commodity that a Scot will give away
freely—to wit, advice. The reason (so our low-
minded critics maintain) that men of my race
are so generous with advice is that it is never
taken. I can well imagine that that fate will
befall many of the suggestions that follow. After
all, if there are nine and sixty ways of inditing
tribal lays, and if every single one of them is
right, there are many more ways than that of
composing a sermon, and each is right, if it is the
best way for the man who adopts it. There is,
surely no art so individual as the art of preaching: and none, therefore, upon which it is more
difficult to give counsel. I remember being
taught to swim by a Spartan father. His
methods were simple, if drastic. He dropped me
into the Clyde and left me to it. Possibly, we

might not depart far from wisdom, if we took the same attitude to the novice in the pulpit. *Experientia docet* in preaching as in other things; and as for the construction of a sermon, *solvitur ambulando* is an applicable Latin tag.

However, a man does not quickly find his own method unless he has considered the devices of other men, even if only to reject them. So it may not be altogether a wasted effort if we spend a little time on suggestions for pulpit preparation.

Now, this subject (like Gaul or a sermon) divides itself into three parts—indirect, semi-direct and direct preparation. And these descend in importance. Indirect preparation is more important than direct in any walk of life. A young doctor's general medical equipment means more to him than his reading of the treatment of measles, directly before he visits his first sick baby. Similarly, the remote preparation that makes a preacher is more vital than the direct preparation which produces a sermon. Wherefore, let us begin with these general considerations, which apply to all pulpit work.

I.

(a) Preaching consists in speaking: and, therefore, learn to speak.

And, here, a word of comfort to the timorous may confidently be given. The art of reasonably coherent and audible public speech may be acquired by anybody, who has a voice, some self-control and an average intelligence. Oratory, of course, is another matter. Orators and poets (for they are first cousins) are born, not made. The mistake preachers sometimes make is to attempt to be orators, when Nature intended them to be speakers only. The orator appears seldom, either in the pulpit or on the platform; but the speaker, being a man who can sustain dignified conversation with a thousand people as easily as with ten, is as common as the average man—if he would only believe it. There is no reason whatever, why the vast majority of us should not be able coherently to address any audience on any ordinary occasion, if we are prepared to take a little trouble at the beginning. Of course, we shall sometimes make fools of ourselves; but these tribulations are only the stepping-stones by which we rise from our stammering selves to the higher things of ease and fluency. The late Lord Morley was, I believe, a failure when he first addressed the House of Commons. As he stood there, nervous and hesitating and almost inaudible, trying to reproduce a carefully prepared essay, his audience imagined him to be yet another instance of those distinguished literary men who are failures in Parliament. But he determined to gain self-control and the art of thinking on his feet; with the result that some years later I heard him gain such a triumph over a huge, hostile audience, as is seldom given to any man to win. What he did, we, in lesser degree, can do. There is no reason at all why most of us should not be quite reasonably good speakers. It is the simplest of all the arts.

But, naturally, skill in this region has to be sought and cultivated. Practice alone will make perfect. The theological student, therefore, has to use all the opportunities, which offer themselves, to speak with a view to learning to speak. It is to provide just such opportunities that college debating clubs exist. Of all the ways in which students waste their time, attendance at college societies is undoubtedly the most useful.

For there a man can find out the method of preparation that is most suitable for himself; he can get rid of self-consciousness; and he can discover that, if he knows anything at all, the impromptu utterance of it is quite easy. In order that they may serve these purposes, student societies should discuss questions which call for the quick play of repartee and wit, of verbal thrust and counter-thrust, rather than those for which men prepare by reading solemn articles in an Encyclopædia. I believe that the habit of having oratorical teams which compete for oratorical championships before judges of oratory is wholly vicious, and is producing a generation of sententious purveyors of verbiage. What a man has to learn is how to clothe his ideas in suitable words on the spur of the moment; how to be natural and moderately confident on his feet, so that his gifts of spontaneity may not be sterilized by nervousness. He learns this by *debating:* and debating is best encouraged by the choice of subjects which are not dealt with in learned tomes. The ideal motion for a college discussion was invented, I believe, by the late J. K. Stephen:—"that this house is of the opinion that the difference between a difference in kind and a difference in degree is a difference in degree and not a difference in kind." You cannot stew up facts from bluebooks on a subject like that, nor does its treatment tend to develop the sesquipedalian style that these oratorical contests seem to encourage.

In addition to college clubs, a student has at his disposal another excellent training-ground— to wit, the open air. In recent years, undergraduates in Britain have taken to visiting industrial centres during their vacations, with a view to speaking on Christian topics at street corners and in public parks. An admirable scheme! If these students do not convince their immediate hearers, they are unconsciously preparing to become much more convincing in their pulpits later on. The open air (if it does not over-strain the vocal chords) teaches a man to keep his voice up, so as to reach the man on the edge of the crowd; it exposes him to interruptions, and so compels him to think as he stands; and it forces him not to be dull, or his audience will silently vanish away. Many of the most effective preachers of to-day learned their art in the open air: and we are foolish if we do not take advantage of so valuable, if so Spartan, a school.

(b) Preaching consists not only in speaking, but in speaking *sense;* and that depends on knowledge and "the full mind," which in their turn depend on reading. Wherefore, take time to read.

Now, this has been repeated to theological students *ad nauseam:* and, anyhow, it is so obvious. What is worse, it is so nearly impossible to follow. The modern minister is the reincarnation of Martha, cumbered with much serving; and, while he is busy here and there, the time for his books has gone. But is it not possible to hope that the generation of ministers that is now appearing will be strong enough to tell their people that nothing short of battle, murder or sudden death will take them out of their studies before lunch? My experience has been that when you go to your office-bearers and take them into your confidence about your work, they, being reasonable citizens, will help you to secure all the quiet that is necessary. And as to all the conferences, reunions and general quasi-religious jamborees, it is always possible to stay away. It is, at any rate, certain that either you are going to find time to read, or one of two things is going to happen—you are going to repeat yourself so much that even the long-suffering patience of the average audience will give way, or you will change a few adjectives in other men's sermons and preach them as your own. "Convey" the wise call it; but the plain English for plagiarism is theft.

But, even at the worst, we have time to ourselves. And let a plea be put in for the use of some of it to keep ourselves familiar with the English classics and, particularly, with the poets. Our reading should not be solely in regions technically theological. Certainly, it should not be directed mainly to next Sunday's work. The reading that creates the full mind is a communing with the great brooders on life, who invite us into their company by the written word, and by their society and intimacy lead us into new lands with wider horizons. Happy men are we, truly, whose work calls us into the comradeship of the great: but foolish, thrice foolish, if, by reason of the fussiness of our time, we neglect their friendship and their wisdom. At least, we can promise to read, let us say, Keats, before we start the latest best-seller—even if it is to be the subject of half the sermons in the town next Sunday. Dr. Whyte's remark to the lady who inquired if he had read some recent hair-raising, ephemeral novel was very *apropos*—"No, Madam, I have not. Have you read Paradise Lost?"

One book, at least, we must study. The Bible is our textbook, and familiarity with it is a *sine qua non.* There are three ways of reading it, and we should omit none of them. We may study it as scholars; we may meditate on it devotionally; and we may read it as literature. My plea is that we should not neglect the last of these. Take a Gospel or a Book of Wisdom, or an Epistle, at a sitting. Buy a Bible with wide margins— the wider the better—and, with a trustworthy commentary at your side and a pencil in your hand, keep your eyes open for three discoveries. First, the homogeneous passage, particularly if it be dramatic in form—such as Isaiah 1: 1-18 or Psalm 2. Second, the striking phrase—such as, "Thy Sons, O Zion, against thy sons, O Greece." And, third, above all, that best of gifts to a preacher, the text that divides itself— such as, "He leadeth me in the paths of righteousness (or, "straight paths") for His Name's sake." * Be careful, when reading the Bible in this way—or, indeed, any other book,—to have that pencil ready. Books, and particularly Bibles, are meant to be written in and marked. If any bibliophile raises shocked hands at this statement, let me remind him of the distressing fate of the man who "roasted not that which he took in hunting." The only result of his day's work was a smell of decaying venison at his back-door, where he dropped the carcass when he came home. Many a man's reading is after that pattern—and all for the lack of a pencil, wherewith to mark his books and make notes. Books are not ornaments, but means for conveying ideas from the author's mind into the reader's, and are to be treated as such.

The written word is, however, not the only source whence comes fullness of mind. "The proper study of mankind is man." The preacher will obtain his best material from his reading

* If a text like this does not "split itself up" before a minister's eyes, he must be asleep. The heads are obvious. (1) The fact of Divine Control—"He leadeth me." (2) The good results of Divine Control—"He leadeth me in straight paths." (3) The reasons for belief in the certainty of the good results—"for His Name's sake." Texts of this sort frequently make the best sermons. They prevent us from using a verse of Scripture as a diving-board into deep waters, where, as the old Scots woman remarked we have "nae groun', but juist gae soomin' aboot."

in human nature. The pastoral and the preaching offices are indubitably intertwined. We must know some people to preach to anybody: and we must know our own people to preach to *them*. And there is no way of getting to know them, but by coming into personal contact with them. Somehow, sometime, the preacher must visit.

Now, here's a pretty problem. It may be all very well in the country. It is usually all very well in a man's first charge, for it will probably be small. But what about the city minister—that hustled jack-of-all trades, who seldom sees his own children? How is the pastoral office to be filled in these days of endless activities? I do not know that there is a more practical question before the Church.

Two points, at any rate, are clear—no man will keep up his pulpit efficiency who is not in constant touch with common folk; and that preacher will be most effective who is the personal friend of all his members. The only practical suggestion I can make is that it is possible, slowly, to get many of your people to come to see you. If you have a really quiet study, and if you make it clear that you welcome them, you will be surprised to what an extent they will take

advantage of the opportunity.   In large congregations, two men are essential—to one of whom
the ordinary "social" round of visiting will be
specially intrusted.   But the preacher, too, must
see his people—especially, the seriously sick and
the young.   The latter can, I think, be easily
persuaded to visit him.   On the other hand, if a
man is to conduct classes as well as to preach
(and this, I think, is vital to-day), he cannot be
expected to call at tea time in every home, once
a year.   He has neither the time nor the physical
strength.   But it will be disastrous if men, starting out on their ministry, think that the pastoral
office is negligible, and the preaching office all
in all.   They are doomed from the beginning to
be bad preachers.   My advice is that we again
take our office-bearers into our confidence, telling
them exactly what we have to do and how long
it takes us to do it.   They are, as aforesaid,
reasonable men, and respond to confidence: and
they can create a tone in our congregations which
prevents unreasonable pastoral demands, and develops a habit of visiting the minister, rather than
of being visited by him.   And we can comfort
ourselves with this reflection—if we go to those

who really need us, we shall go to all our people in due time.*

One object of pastoral care must never be neglected—the pastorless pastor himself. He needs his quiet hour, when the door of his chamber is shut and he is alone. His care of himself, in the midst of the severe and subtle temptations of the ministerial life, demands the solitary place of remembrance. His preaching, too, requires him to face the facts, especially the harsh facts, of his own life, and to discover the spiritual meaning of his own experience. He is not likely to "give draughts restorative" to his hearers unless they "well from the deeps of his own soul." So find time—make time—to brood. "I am still a slow study," wrote Stevenson, "and sit for a long while silent on my eggs. In conscious thought, that is the only method. Macerate your subject, let it boil slow, then take the lid off and look in, and there is your stuff—good or bad." If these are the processes by which a novelist and

* Our little plan, which is adopted in my own congregation, may be helpful to others. We have little cards, on which there is printed a message of greeting and sympathy. On these cards, the sermon texts for the day are written, and each card is signed by me. They are then tied with ribbon to a flower from the church and taken to all the sick and aged, after the morning service, by young ladies. It is a custom that seems to be appreciated.

essayist brings forth his work, how much more are they necessary for the preacher, who must explore the recesses of his own soul? It is not easy to compel ourselves to seek the quiet place in the quiet hour. But we must.

(c) Preaching consists not only in speaking sense, but in speaking that particular sense which the occasion demands. Therefore, in addition to the full mind, it requires the ready mind.

Now, the basis of a ready mind is memory; and aspiring preachers will early cultivate that faculty. Of all our faculties, none responds more to cultivation. Amazing instances of the extent to which it can develop will occur to us all. I knew a man who could repeat the whole of the Anglican burial service, because, twenty years before, the position he then occupied often necessitated his attendance at funerals conducted by Anglican clergy; and yet he had never made any conscious effort to learn it. The power to deliver a long address *verbatim* after writing it, and with only one re-reading, is reasonably common. It is a mistake, I think, to trust to a power of that sort in the pulpit. Memorized sermons, as a rule, betray themselves. But it is no mistake to cultivate memory, so as to have the resources of your reading at hand when you want them. So begin at once—you cannot begin too soon—and learn poetry and devotional passages from King James' version every morning before breakfast. Let me make one poor boast—I did that every morning for five years in my student days, and I have been thankful for it ever since. In addition to giving a store of knowledge, to be drawn on at command, it does much to improve us in devotional speech: and, anyhow, if you do it, you will look back on yourself with a certain satisfaction in the time to come.

II.

The second type of preparation we have termed semi-direct. By that I mean those pre-arrangements and plannings which keep us ahead of our work. Remember how much we have to do. Two sermons, a week-night address and a Bible-class instruction (or their modern equivalent), together with outside speeches and lectures, keep us busy. If our work is not planned in advance, we shall collapse.

Fortunately, to some degree, our work tends to plan itself. We shall be very foolish if we do not follow the Christian Year, and thereby in association with our fellow-Christians, find that our subjects are frequently chosen for us. The great festivals and the Lenten season are now commonly remembered in our churches: but we might go further and also observe Advent—those four Sundays before Christmas, when we should call the attention of our people to the "solemnities,"—and such a tender day as All Souls' Day at the end of October. The advantage of the Church Year is not only that it compels us to preach on the whole round of the Christian faith, but that it determines our choice of a subject for half the Sundays of the year and thereby saves us that painful search which makes Tuesday so often a depressing day.

And, I hope, the old fashion of "courses" is not going to be given up. They are helpful to everybody—to the minister, as safeguards against casualness in study, and to the people, for they are assured of some sustained instruction. They should not, indeed, continue too long. When I was a boy I heard sermons on the Epistle of James for nearly ten consecutive months, and have not been enthusiastic about that book since. Six or seven sermons are numerous enough for

any course; and courses, following on each other,
should vary in type. You can have the detailed
(the "pre-Raphaelite," if you prefer it) course,
in which you go carefully down a few verses,
word by word. That is the way to treat the
opening passages of Ephesians or Colossians.
But a series such as that should be followed by
an "impressionist" course, in which you select the
"high-lights" of a book, or give a bird's eye view
of the teaching of a prophet. You will find
Ezekiel excellent material for that kind of treatment. And, once in a while, you can vary it by
having a purely theological, or topical, series.
Try some consecutive sermons, sometime, on the
doctrine of the Cross, or on the Christian vocabu-
lary, choosing great words such as Sin, Faith,
Redemption, Life, Love.

At any rate, do not begin a series until, say,
three months after you have decided upon it.
Use the interval to get the general scheme clear
in your mind, and to discover where you can lay
hold of your material, when you come to working
out details. For only so will you be defended
from the hand-to-mouth methods, which weaken
so many ministers. Profanely searching the
Scriptures for a text on Saturday morning is

the precursor of many a ministerial failure. We are not likely to be inspired when we are desperate.

And as we plan subjects far ahead, so also plan each week ahead. If we are in the middle of a series, or approaching a festival, one sermon is settled. We shall be well advised to get the other subject selected as early in the week as possible. For, thereby, we save ourselves subconscious worry, and have all our work to brood on for the maximum length of time. The question of choosing our second text is not always an easy one: and the following suggestions may be helpful. Special occurrences, in the national or parochial life, are the most obvious starting points in the choice of a subject. If none of these has happened, very likely some immediately previous experience, either personal or pastoral, will set the mind working. Take a little time to search through memory to see if God has not been teaching some particular lesson in the preceding week. If nothing suggests itself, turn to your marked Bible, until a verse, that you have formerly noted, fastens itself on the mind. Most of our second sermons are, I suppose, chosen in this way: but, you observe, it implies that we have a well-

marked Bible to turn to. If all else fails, then
take a block of Scripture,—a parable or a com-
pleted argument in an Epistle, or a Bible character, and force yourself to make a sermon.
Sometimes, of course, a discourse produced in
this way will be rather an artisan affair: but you
will often be surprised and delighted to discover
how the mind begins to waken up, and produce
work as good as you can do. If you have a gift
that way, the selection of a Bible character is
probably the most promising. But be sure you
have the gift for that type of preaching, before
indulging in it overmuch. Some men are extraordinarily good at it—and a very fine kind of work
is can be. Most of us, however, should only go
to it when we are in the mood: otherwise we shall
produce discourses of the "when, where, what"
sort—when Moses lived, where Moses lived, and
what Moses did when he lived. In the arid moments, we are safest to stick to a passage of
Scripture, such as a parable, which we can try to
explain. In any case, however bad the going may
be, we should be able to say "a poor thing—*but
mine own*." Plagiarism has been defined as that
degree of dependence upon another man's work,
which would make us ashamed if we suddenly

saw him, while we were preaching.   May none of us ever experience shame of that sort.

III.

Thus, at last, we arrive at direct preparation. Let us put down our suggestions, *seriatim,* as they come.

(a) Paraphrase your passage or text and define the main terms in it. Be precise and clear as to meaning—and keep an especially alert eye on such words as "law," "natural" and "justice."

(b) Take a large sheet of paper, and jot down any ideas which the text suggests to you—anyhow. Do not trouble about their logical sequence. Your business at present is to get your "apperceptive mass" moving. It does not matter what comes, provided it has some relation to the subject in the text: down with it.

(c) Get a system of numbering heads and subheads, which you always use. It should not be too elaborate, but (to my mind) it should provide for quite a series of subdivisions. Personally, I use I, i, a, 1, in that order. As a rule, the first three are sufficient. Their chief use is in arranging the ideas that have been flung in confusion on your sheet of paper.

(d) Set to and number these ideas accordingly, seeking strength to cultivate the grace of rejection. It is hard to leave out a pretty quotation: but, unless it forces its way in, keep it out.

(e) Copy out, on a clean sheet of paper, the ideas you have retained, in the order in which you have numbered them—writing your sub-heads with a wider margin. The same arrangement on the paper, as well as the same numbering, greatly helps memory, if your memory is a visual one.

When you have done that, the outline of your sermon will be complete, and it will fall into a mold something like this:—

```
Introd.
            i.
                    a.
                    b.
            ii.
            iii.
            iv.
   I.
            i.
            ii.
   II.
            i.
                    a.
                    b.
            ii.
            iii.
            iv.
                    a.
                    b.
```

III.

    i.

        a.
        b.
        c.

    ii.

        a.
        b.
        c.

    iii.

        a.
        b.
        c.

Concl.

Then, if you like, you can write the whole thing out at top speed: or you can put the outline in your sermon-case, thankful that another job of work is finished. Personally, I do the latter.

Now, you observe that the three points of hard work are when we are defining our text, squeezing our minds for related ideas, and, finally, arranging and discarding. Our chief difficulty is how to secure that all our own resources will be at our disposal, when we are at the second process. The collection of references in a card-index, or on a wide-margined Bible, is helpful, no doubt—though I have never found a system entirely satisfactory. But one thing I have found very profitable—namely, to talk over the subject with an understanding friend.

Conversation tends to clarity and logical progression: and it sets two apperceptive masses moving in place of one. The difficulty, of course, is that it implies a partner. Well, there are such things as secretaries, or brother ministers, or even wives. At any rate, I am certain that many a sermon would be strengthened, and many a bad argument prevented, if a minister had a chance to discuss his thoughts before he preached them.

It may be of interest to students to see what a sermon form of that kind looks like when the notes are filled in. The numbering printed above is that of the morning sermon preached in Old St. Andrew's Church, Toronto, on Sunday, May 23rd, 1927. It was not written with any thought of being used as an illustration in this book, but it happens to be a good enough instance of the notes of an ordinary morning sermon—fashioned in the way I am recommending. I have resisted the temptation to alter it for publication, and print it exactly as I took it into the pulpit with me. I had it in the Bible in the page *after* the one on which the text occurred so as to be able to find it quickly if my memory failed; but nothing untoward like that happened. Notes such as these fill three sides of an ordinary double

sheet of note paper. On the fourth side, I enter
the text, the lessons read, and the date and service of preaching. I find that, with notes of
this kind, I can recapture a sermon even after
many years. This particular discourse did not
prepare "smoothly." I had to recast it twice,
and students may obtain some entertainment by
tightening its links and generally improving it.
The text was "Blessed are they who have not
seen, and yet have believed," from John 20:29—
a "proper passage" for this season of the year,
lying between the Resurrection and Ascension.

Introd.

    i. We must all feel sympathy with doubting Thomas,
       because—
       a. He was so much in accord, intellectually, with
          our time, and because
       b. He was the possessor of an unfortunate tem-
          perament—pessimistic and melancholic: for
          which he was no more to blame than for a
          tendency to rheumatism or tuberculosis.
   ii. Moreover, he was a very fine fellow—loyal in
       spite of melancholia, hopeful in spite of dread.
       There will be a lot like him in heaven.
  iii. In this story, we see his sort symbolised as satis-
       fied at last. The 'sorrowful spirit' transmuted
       into joy in the perfected kingdom.

iv. The incident is specially significant for the generalism to which it gives rise.

The risen Christ is looking forward to the Church that is to be and foreseeing its difficulties.

No literal proof: no seeing of wounds. Nothing but His spiritual presence and power.

And of them He says "Blessed are they. . . . "

Blessed are they who may not walk by sight, but succeed in walking by faith.

I. *Religious faith is ultimately trust in a particular Person: for Christian faith that Person is Christ.*

    i. It involves
        a. Intellectual assent to His teaching.
        b. Practical obedience to His commands.
    ii. It implies the possibility of mistake.

It would not be trust if there were not reasonable grounds for thinking that conceivably, in so trusting, we are wrong.

There is an element of *risk* in faith.

II. *The Regions of Risk in Faith.*

    i. We have to choose, often, between different goods.
        a. The denial of either means the denial of a full life.
        b. And we *may* be "martyrs by mistake."
            e. g., the clash between duty and happiness. The denial of the latter means the denial of elasticity and buoyancy. In the perfect life, God shall wipe away *these* tears, at any rate.
    ii. Or, to take the same point from another angle, there is the clash between our duty to ourselves and to our neighbours.

"Thou shalt love thy neighbour *as* thyself".

It is that "as" that creates all the trouble.

iii. Further, there is the clash between our ideal of duty and our own power.

On the one hand "I know I ought".

On the other "I am sure I can't".

Is a clash like that God's will; or are we mistaken about the "ought"?

iv. And, finally, there is the perplexity due to the fact that the harsher demands of right are often caused by

a. Other people's sin, or

b. Their *inevitable* imperfection.

The former has nothing to do with God: the latter seems to make Him an imperfect worker.

e. g.

under (a) a daughter with an unreasonable, selfish parent.

under (b) a wife, or a husband, with a mate that was born a "mollusc".

What *is* the right thing to do in these circumstances? At any rate, there is plenty of room for walking by faith.

III. *The Call of Christ to take the risk.*

This is explicit, unhesitating, clarion-like.

i. It contains

a. "Seek ye *first*. . . "

b. The path of search is the path of the Cross.

c. "Follow *Me*".

There is no question about the Christ-demand: either in precept or example. When in doubt, listen to the inner voice that calls to self-denial.

ii. Wherefore, our duty is

a. Cultivate the ear that is sensitive to the "long, low note of sacrifice".

b. If we would satisfy our minds, let us "universalise our conduct".

    c. When things are bad, turn sharp into His society. "Straight to His presence get me and reveal it . . . "

  iii. If we do that last, certain results follow.

    a. A feeling that we must not let Him down, and of utter shame, when we remember that we have done so.

    b. A compelling thought that His loveliness must be right.

    c. A remembrance of the results that followed on His own loyalty to the inner voice.

    After all, He does not ask us to go where He feared to lead. Our worst is but a shadow of His pain.

Concl. Thus, at least, the heart grows warm again; we feel the gallantry of "Stand thou on that side . . . " And then, in assenting, there touches us, "with a ripple and a radiance", the promise of His renewal—when at last pain shall yield to peace for those who, having been faithful, are blessed in their Heavenly Father's realm. Amen.

IV.

There remains only the vexed question of delivery, about which I propose to say very little, because everybody—in pulpit and in pew alike—has his mind made up. The verdict is in favour of the spoken and against the read sermon: and it is no use arguing about it.

But I will allow myself the freedom of recording my opinion that, for a sustained minis-

try, really good reading is the best preaching.
Donne, Newman and Chalmers, to mention no
others, were all readers; and though, doubtless,
it was "fell reading yon," nevertheless it was
reading. A read sermon is more likely to be
proportionate in its parts and to achieve a true
literary distinction. It is at once a deterrent to
fatal fluency, and a lessener of nervous strain.
But—and here's the rub—it is not easy to write
a *sermon* as distinct from an essay; and to *preach*
a written sermon, as distinct from reading it, is
very difficult. If you are going .to read, you
must write in the spoken style. As your pen flies
over the paper, you should have your congregation before your eyes. Things are going well,
if you find your left hand gesticulating in the
air as you write. If, in addition, you are one of
these masters of voice, who can follow a manuscript without developing a pulpit accent, then
do not let anyone stop you from reading. But
most of us cannot do that. We lose spontaneity;
we become monotonous and wooden; and our in-
effectiveness finally drives us, willy-nilly, to extempore preaching. And if that is your best
method, do not stop at half-way houses. Memo-
rising is far too great a strain, and it has the

appearance of spontaneity without the reality—
despite the example of the great French preachers, who adopted this method. Elaborate notes
break the connection between speaker and audience, if they are constantly being referred to.
The best way is to get your outline photographed
in your mind; put it somewhere in the Bible,
where you cannot see it but can find it if the
weather gets heavy; and then step back in the
pulpit, trust in Providence, and heave ahead.

But that does not mean that we should not
write sermons at all. On the contrary, I think
we should write out one a week in the earlier
part of our ministries, if only as a discipline and
to cultivate a literary style. Further, our preparation should be more, and not less thorough,
than if we are going to read. We ought to know
our work so well by Saturday at mid-day that
we can give Saturday evening to recreation, and
Sunday morning, after one glance through our
sermon notes, to the preparation of our prayers
and to the quietening of our hearts, so that
with slow, unhurried steps we may walk into our
pulpits to utter the solemn words which mark
the beginning of a noble enterprise—"Let us
worship God."

CHAPTER V.

THE TEACHING METHODS OF OUR LORD.

BEFORE we leave this matter of preaching, it may be well to spend a little time to glance at the methods which were used by Him who manifestly was the Teacher sent from God. But, first, it is necessary to enter a certain *caveat*. It is not possible for us to copy Jesus: His methods, like His message, are His own. The question which simple, devout souls sometimes put to themselves in a difficulty—"what would Jesus do?"—is a question which does credit to their piety, but not always to their intelligence. For it assumes that only that which Jesus would do is fit for us to do. You cannot conceive Him as being engaged in the vast majority of the specialized activities of modern society, such as playing in an orchestra, or poring over the minutiæ of scholarship. Indeed, you cannot imagine Him doing anything other than that on which He actually spent His life. The proper question to put to ourselves is, not "What would Jesus do?" but "What would Jesus have me to do?" For He had a baptism to be baptised with, and was pained when His friends did not realize that He must be about His Father's business; and, therefore, was excluded from many of the quite honourable interests of ordinary men.

Reflections such as these bear upon the question of His example as a preacher. Because He was unique, His methods may well be unique also. Seeing that our teaching is so largely derivative, while His was direct, our methods may be expected to be different from His. Further, Jesus was not confined to a settled pastorate, which calls for the continuous repetition of the same religious ideas to the same group: and He was free to break through the trammels of convention, inevitably associated with an established organization.

At the same time, He was *the* Preacher; and it is surely seemly to study the manner, as well as the matter, of His message. We may, thereby, find guidance in regions that are full of pitfalls. At least, we may catch something of the spirit of confidence and of reverence, which determined not only what He said, but how He said it.

Wherefore, let us set down, as they come, some of the characteristics of the form of His teaching, which leap to the eye as we turn the pages of the records.

I.

Our Lord evidently held that preaching was intended to give vitality by means of illumination.   Therein, He must have been in startling contrast to the doctors of the synagogue, who, as they taught, bound fresh burdens, grievous to be borne, on the shoulders of their hearers. Legality rather than vitality was their object; vitality rather than legality was Christ's.   He was more concerned with the "how" of living than with the "what" of it: or, if that be a false antithesis, He felt that man's chief need was not enlightenment as to the law, but power to keep the law he knew.   So He showed men God, and told them about His willingness to give them the Holy Spirit.   When people left Christ's presence they did not shake their heads and say, "How high is this hill that we have to climb," but "We believe that we shall really be able to climb this hill, steep as it is; and, what's more, it will be worth it, when we get to the top."   A point, this

surely, for all preachers today, or any other day.
It is hope that saves—the hope of power, through
which we may be more than conquerors. We
shall be poor ambassadors for Christ, if we do
not make this note dominant in our preaching.

From this general observation, we can proceed
to enumerate the characteristics oi the method
which Jesus employed to show, not the weight
of our burdens, but the power by which we can
bear them.

1. On the whole, and in His intimate discourses, He worked upwards rather than down-
wards—from an instance to a principle, from the
particular to the general, from the seen to the
Unseen, from man to God. Instances innumer-
able suggest themselves. Starting from a lost
coin, a grain of wheat, or a hungry boy, He
worked up till He left His hearers secure in the
love of God. The preaching of the synagogue
reversed this order. It began with a general
rule, such as the rule not to labour on the Sabbath, and worked down to particular applications,
which only made life more difficult for working
folk. Protestant preaching has often tended to
the same method. Taking an abstract proposi-
tion as the starting point, it worked down from

an application of the general to the particular,
and thence to the man who happened to be sitting in the pew—probably, and not unnaturally,
asleep. The method of Jesus, surely, is more
likely to keep attention and to leave hope in its
train. Let men start with what they know—
let them contemplate "every common bush," and,
before they have finished, they may discover that
it is a burning bush, "aflame with God."

2. And then, the *freshness* of those lovely
stories, in which He so gently lifted men up from
the things around them to the thought of God's
love. They have the flavour of a morning in
May,—"a morning at seven, dew-pearled." To
hear them, after hearing the prosy disquisitions of
the scribes, must have been like stepping out of a
musty room into God's fresh air in a Highland
strath. They are akin to the flowers, and the
grass, and the sunlight. No wonder that the
common people heard Him gladly. Is it not true
that we have turned our churches into the musty
room and made them the direct descendants of
the synagogue? And is it beyond our range to
bring in something of the sweet air and the danc-
ing light, into which the teaching of Jesus always
seems to lead us?

3. The *naturalness* (it is a poor word, but I can think of no better) of the forms He used leaps to the eye as spontaneously as their freshness. He is true to Himself, all the time. Here is no copy, and no copyist. As the lark ascending sings out its own heart, so Jesus teaches in the manner that natively springs from His own mind.

4. The *simplicity* of it all equally delights and amazes us. Anybody can understand that story about the boy that went away. No old woman of the isles was ever in doubt about its meaning. But it is the simplicity of depth—like some clear water, on which the sunlight falls. No wayfaring man need fail to comprehend: but the wise bringing all their learning, will never be able to say they have exhausted its riches.

It is, I think, due to the fact that Jesus worked upwards, that simplicity so marks His teaching. He begins so near to ordinary life. Children at play, Pilate's folly, a sleepy citizen in bed—all these are part and parcel of the ordinary images of everyday. No one was puzzled by them. Perhaps, too, the platform which He used was a help—for He spoke mostly in the open air: and His manner as He spoke assisted, also. There

is a delightful picture by a Russian artist of
the scene at the close of the story of the Good
Samaritan, when Jesus is putting, to a badly
trapped lawyer, the question "Which now was
neighbour unto him that fell among thieves?"
Our Lord is portrayed as standing not far from
the roadside, surrounded by a little group of people, mostly insignificant to look at. Along the
track, a young woman is passing on a mule: her
veil is drawn back and her eyes, grave and searching, are focused on the Master's face. Pressing
against Jesus are several little children. Two
hold His hands, and He is swinging with them,
as He talks. Others are clutching His robe;
one, indeed, is adventurously trying to climb up;
and another, a tiny fellow, is rubbing his fat, little
knuckles into tearful eyes, because he cannot get
past the bigger boys. At the back of the crowd,
the lawyer is fingering his beard, a delightful
figure of perplexity, while Jesus watches him
with a twinkling smile in His eyes. It is a curiously convincing picture. That was the way,
we feel, that Jesus taught: and perhaps it helps
to explain why He could keep, apparently so
easily, in touch with life as it is. I wonder if

we should get on better, if we made the lake-
side and the field our pulpit?

5. One point in His method, at any rate, is
indubitable. He disdained neither the use of
imagination or *humour*. Nobody, obviously, can
deny that He allowed His mind to soar imagin-
atively where it would; but there are those who
to deny that He permitted the humourous to
sparkle through His words. A great Scottish
scholar of the last generation is alleged to have
said that he could not conceive of Jesus as smiling, and, far less, laughing. Well, there are
smiles and smiles: and that Jesus smiled at the
humourous, and that He caused His hearers to
break into delighted laughter, seems to me to be
written clearly in the records. The picture, which
some of the parables create in the mind, have all
the elements of humour in them. Can you not see
that sleepy citizen, with tousled hair, coming
down in his dressing-gown, to grunt out a refusal
to what he thought a perfectly idiotic request for
the loan of a loaf? If he does not move us to a
smile, the word-portrait of the snubbed "climber"
certainly will. You can see him (or her), stout
and overdressed, coming back with a very red
face, after the unsuccessful attempt to grab a

seat at the head table. Dr. Glover points out
that the idea of swallowing a camel must have
been highly diverting to simple Eastern people,
who knew all about camels, and their humps and
hoofs and general rampageousness. The fact is
that we have to modernize the parables, before
we catch their full flavour. We must think of the
sleepy citizen as a town councillor in our own
town, and the snubbed guest at the wedding as a
local aspirer for social honours, if we would realize the ripples of laughter with which the original
audience heard them. But when we make them
contemporaneous, we are in no doubt about their
occasional humour. Take the best instance of
all—the instance of the lost coin. Jesus was surrounded by one of the normal crowds, and was
greatly stirred to speak to them directly of God's
love. As usual, His eye ran over them, as He
sought inspiration, and suddenly it fell on a
countryman at the back, with his crook in his
hand. In a moment the Master was off, speaking
straight to the shepherd, and leaping upwards,
from his care for his lost sheep, to the Heavenly
Father's care for His children. When the story
was finished, the Lord's eye fell on another face
—the determined-looking, competent face of a

housewife: and it lit up with a charming gleam
as He perceived another line of approach. Now,
make the scene contemporary. Imagine it in
Scotland—dare we say, in Aberdeen? Scots are
supposed to carry on and adorn the thriftiness
of the Hebrews; and Scotswomen are alleged
to be specially aware of the value of sixpence.
Notice, particularly, the pointed adverb "diligently." "What woman among you who has
lost a three-penny bit, would not sweep *diligently?*" Of course, the people laughed. Certainly any Greeks that were present did. How
could they help it? But He did not leave the
matter there. His mind afire, He swept on to
the story of the wayward son—a story, the music
of which will echo in men's hearts to the end of
time. The humour was but a stepping-stone to
beauty and truth.

6. You notice, further, how He *emphasized
a single idea at a time*. The details of the
parables are, I believe, often embroideries to the
story: and the work of commentators, who would
extract theological meaning out of every turn of
phrase, is often a labour lost. We need to look
for the one thought which Jesus was at that time
engaged in conveying. When we discover it,

we are sometimes startled by the daring with which it was emphasized.   In the instance of the parable of the prodigal son, there are apparently no limits to the lengths He will go to impress on us God's longing for our return.   A father, leaning over a gate at the end of a farm lane, watching the road every evening in the gloaming; and, at last, running to meet the tattered figure of his son and holding him to his heart as he kisses him, is a tender and human figure: but it is a strange image for Almighty God.   Yet that is the image which Jesus chose for the most intimate of all His teachings on the Father.   He was evidently anxious that we should believe that God loves us.   At any rate, He spared no vigour of emphasis in His telling.

7.   Further, His skill in *repetition* is easy to discern.   In Luke 15 the same idea is repeated thrice, though in the third statement of it a new point of teaching is added.   The active longing of God is displayed in all three parables, but in the last of them He reminds us that a son is more than a sheep or a coin.   The latter are simply found; but the former must himself say "I will arise and go"—a vital point for preaching. Even with this addition, however, the repetition

is very skilful. Jesus made the same point three times in one short conversation, and no one was wearied.

8. And, finally, there are the related characteristics of His *"surefootedness,"* and His *spiritual anxiety.* In the divine region where man has lost his way, Jesus walks confidently, as in a country that He knows well—a country that is His own. It was a perception of this sure sense of direction that made people say that He spake with authority and not as the scribes. And this spiritual awareness makes more poignant the anxiety that rings through His "Verily, verily," and quivers in His voice as He pleads that those who have ears may hear.

II.

What, then, has all this to do with us? Does it bear any relation to our humble work? Surely, in three ways it gives us hints as to certain ideals at which we should aim.

1. First, let us learn to be ourselves, when we preach—ourselves and not another. Pale copies of some famous preacher are all too common, and as ineffective as they are frequent. An

unfortunate by-product of the impact of a great personality upon lesser minds is the creation of a school of mimics, rather than disciples. We all have known little quasi-replicas of Joseph Parker or Ian Maclaren, who reproduced the mannerisms, without the flame, of their models. It is, of course, impossible to avoid being influenced by a master of the craft: but a man must be on his guard against submerging his own personality. For that reason it is not, I think, advisable to read too many sermons by other men. Apart from the danger of direct plagiarism, there is the subtle risk of being coerced into using forms and attempting methods that are effective only when allied to a distinct, sharply outlined type of mind. The stately robes of a great orator change painfully into cap and bells when assumed by smaller men. "To thine own self be true" is sound advice for a preacher. A man's mental stature will increase if he studies great literature: but, at each stage of his development, his expression should be native to himself. If we try to make religious truths clear in the pulpit in the way in which we make them clear to ourselves (having due regard, of course, to the *decorum* of a church), we shall not go far wrong. At any rate, Christ's example is clear: do not imitate, but be yourself.

2. Second, we should cultivate diligently the use of imagery with a view to repetition. We are not far off the mark if we say that preaching is the art of saying the same thing over and over again without wearying our hearers. After all, the main religious ideas are both simple and few. It is their illustration and application that are varied: and we have to call in all our resources of imagination, if our work is to keep fresh. We need to develop the "homiletic eye," which is acute to perceive material for our work wherever we go, and finds sermons in stones, books in the running brooks. Almost everything we can learn, or see, will be grist to our mill some day: and the variety of our preaching will depend on our alertness of vision at all times. If we possess the seeing eye, we need never retail old sermons, but (as Dr. Parker used to say) we shall preach "the same good new one, again and again."

3. Thirdly, and particularly, we must learn to use rightly the humourous and the *outré*. To be rightly guided here is of the utmost importance in these days: for many a time the modern pulpit ought to be ashamed of its vagaries. Any

kind of harlequin-work seems to be justified, if
it can gather a crowd. As if that were any
test! A clown will always gather a crowd—
for a while, especially a clown in God's house.
Human nature responds to the bizarre. The
real test is whether a crowd can be *kept*—and,
while kept, can be increasingly interested in
religion. Against all mere sensation-mongering
and vaudeville tricks decent men will set their
faces like flints. But that does not mean that
humour is not to play through some sermons, or
that an unconventional man has to be conven-
tional in his methods. We have all been sorry
that some of our friends are so wooden in the
pulpit, when we know them to be vivacious and
quick-witted talkers by their own firesides.
Many of the strongest preachers, alike of the
past and the present, startle staid congregations
by what they say and how they say it: indeed,
if more of our flocks were surprised out of their
decorous inattention, it would be better for all
concerned. Our problem is where, and how, to
draw the line between the *outré,* which is reverent
at its core, and that which is blatantly vulgar.

The example of Jesus, whose methods must
have been so startling to the standardized people

of His own day, helps us here for three good
reasons: He loved the lovely; He entirely forgot
Himself in His message; and He related all His
work directly to the supreme end of the Kingdom.   True cultivation of self, forgetfulness of
self and absorption in a noble purpose form a
triple bondage which spell perfect freedom.   As
is the Master so should the servants be.   If His
spirit is in us, we likewise shall be bound and
likewise free.   In particular, if we are natural
rebels against the decorous, there is the more
need for us to have our securities within ourselves against the indecorous.   With that in view,
we must endeavour to develop our love of beauty
in every way we can, adding music and art to
literature and nature.   The vulgarians of the
pulpit are, if they only knew it, confessing their
lack of liberal education.   They obviously do
not seek the society of the masters of words, or
sound, or colour.   None who frequently betakes
himself to that kind of comradeship can ever in-
troduce the banal or the grotesque into God's
worship.   Still more, vulgarity in preaching is
a proof of self-centredness.   Much that jars in
pulpit work is due to the fact that the preacher
is self-consciously trying to be "clever."   He is

anxious, not that men should be helped to live, but that they should think the speaker smart. A temptation of that sort is constantly stabbing at us—often when we are least aware of it. Wherefore, we need to lose ourselves in the purpose to which the Lord dedicated His life. The dream of the kingdom—ah! that is a dream, indeed! When the battlements of the City loom, however faintly, through the mists, the tempter with his mean allurements slinks away defeated. Be passionate with Christ—and then be free!

The fact is that the métier of the preacher is its own defense against unworthy forms of work. For a preacher is in part a physician and in part a teacher; and neither of these is vulgar, when he is engaged on his work. The physician is a fighter against disease—and, while a fighter may be lighthearted, there is a gravity behind the sparkle of his eyes. And a teacher is, or ought to be, a lover of truth: and a lover of the true may be uncouth, but he is never unseemly. He may permit humour, wit and gaiety; he may call in the aid of the unexpected and the startling; but the truth, whose servant he is, lends him its own dignity. So keep in view the ends of preaching: and then be, and say, and do what you will.

Above all, there remains the Master's example in authority. He spoke because he knew. Here, at the best, His servants follow Him afar off. But the preachers of His evangel must know something for themselves. It is the love which has touched their own hearts which they desire to commend to those who hear them. And that knowledge should grow from more to more, until men believe our words because they believe that we spoke of that which our own eyes have seen. Preaching, finally, depends on life. Even the seemliness of its form depends on life. It all comes to this—a preacher should be a Christian gentleman.

CHAPTER VI.

IN the Church of the Reformation, the Sacraments are two only in number—Baptism and Holy Communion: and of these two the latter is, in common *parlance, the* Sacrament, which explains the title given to this chapter. But, while we shall confine ourselves to the Lord's Supper in this discussion, I would not have us think of Baptism as other than a singularly important celebration in the worship of the Church. Its symbolism is far-reaching, when it reminds us that men must die to live, and that even the purest of us all needs cleansing. Moreover, in Churches such as our own, who hold to the baptism of infants, it ought to be a marked *churchly* occasion, at which the members of the Christian community take vows to create an atmosphere in which the growth of the child into Christian faith and discipleship shall be as natural as the opening of flowers to the sun. Consequently,

baptism should (except in cases where danger
to health is involved) always be a part of public
worship before the whole congregation, who, by
standing, assent to the vows which are laid upon
them as well as upon the parents. Ministers
should be firm with nervous parents and refuse to
baptize at home or at any other time than at the
main diet of worship. After all, it is usually
the father who is timorous, and too much respect
need not be paid to his nerves. If the health
of either the mother or the child is such as to
make the journey to the church impossible or
dangerous, the minister should take an official
representative of the church with him and should
encourage the parents to invite as many relatives
who are members of the church as is convenient.
We want to get away from the pernicious, magical idea that the sprinkling of water and the saying of a formula is going to make any difference
to the child *per se:* and in its place we need to
emphasize the noble conception of the reception
of a little friend into the Society of which the
Friend of little children is the Head—a Society
which is rededicating itself for the child's sake.
The particular vows should only be taken by
members of the Church. If both the father and

mother are not members, someone else, who is in a position to do it, must take them in their place. Unless some responsible person is qualified to take the vows, baptism should not be administered. The christening of children promiscuously breeds superstition.

I.

The Sacrament of the Lord's Supper is, however, our main concern, for it is the central act of worship of the Christian Church. There are, unfortunately, good grounds for believing that a re-emphasis of its supreme importance is badly needed. Quite alarming statements are made by men who are in a position to know, as to the casual, and indeed culpable, manner in which it is sometimes celebrated—if it is celebrated at all. We cannot be too explicit: the Church is founded on both the Word *and* the Sacraments: and a Christian Society which neglects either, thereby ceases to be a Church. The Quakers and the Salvation Army both form admirable Christian Societies; but neither administers the Sacraments, and, consequently and quite rightly, does not claim to be a Church. Men, who occupy

responsible positions, sometimes make it clear
that they have only the vaguest idea what Holy
Communion purports to be and do: and if they
are the authentic voice of the Protestantism of
the New World we need not be surprised at
reading articles telling us that Protestantism is
breaking up.

For the Lord's Supper was founded by Christ
Himself: it is continued at His own request: and
it has become the chief of all the *ordinary* means
of grace. It is, in the beautiful words of the
Scottish liturgy, "singular medicine for sick
souls." Dr. Robert Bruce, who was minister of
St. Giles' in Edinburgh in critical days nearly
two centuries ago, uttered a good word about it
when he said, "whereas by the Word I do get
hold of Christ as it were by my finger and thumb,
in the Sacrament I get hold of Him by my
haill hand." In dropping to modern, jejune
thoughts of it as a mere service of remembrance,
which can be conducted by anybody, anywhere,
or can be omitted at pleasure, we are wandering
far from the Reformation. Luther or Calvin,
or even Zwingli, would have made short work of
the disseminators of all such views. It should
never be forgotten how rich was the sacramental

doctrine of all the Reformers, who held their opinions because they found them in Scripture. They would all agree upon some form of teaching the Real Presence. "The only difference between us and the Anglo-Catholics," as somebody said recently, "is that we believe the Real Presence to be intensely spiritual and they believe the Spiritual Presence to be intensely real." While that may be an understatement of the position of the Anglo-Catholics, it is precisely accurate in regard to our own, unless we are degenerate sons of the Reformation.

Further, inasmuch as the Table offers a "singular medicine for *sick* souls," it is spread for *sinners:* and is, consequently, the supreme comfort-occasion in our worship. There is a beautiful little tale, well-known to Scottish ears, of an Edinburgh professor, familiarly known as Rabbi Duncan, who, once, when he was celebrating Communion, noticed that an old woman in the front pews, after having received the Bread, had refused the Wine. He stepped down from his place and, taking the Cup from the elder's hands, went back with it, saying "Tak' it, wumman, tak' it: it's *for* sinners." And she took, drank and was thankful.* The implications of this for ministers in inviting people to partake will be dealt with later: but, meantime, we gain from it an understanding of how far the Sacrament goes to meet our deepest needs. For the Sacrament is the symbolized offer of pardon, cleansing and power. It is the Christian gospel gathered into a sign. It speaks directly to the afraid and the forsaken. It is, itself, a channel of that grace which excludes none but seeks all. And a Church which fails to take this thing seriously is a Church which has within it the seeds of decay.

II.

Let us, then, spend some time in endeavouring to discover the meanings of a service of such associations. On our Reformed principles, we must turn to the Scriptures, which are our "rule" for faith, and extract from them the various passages which tell of the institution of the Sacrament and its attendant circumstances. When we have made a harmony of these, we have before us all the material we possess on which to

* Curiously enough, I had an exactly similar experience with a young soldier in France in the war. I whispered Rabbi Duncan's words in his ear, with a similar result.

base our doctrine. We must take the records at their face value. Critical inquiry throws no doubt on the statement that Jesus declared "This is my body," as He broke the bread: and, therefore, we have an unquestioned basis for sacramental teaching. But we are not concerned with critical questions. Working on the agreed ground of the authority of the Synoptics and the Pauline Epistles, we seek to discover the teaching that is in them all, put together. We have only four passages, of four verses each, to consider—apart from one or two phrases elsewhere, which give us the setting of the Supper. These four occur in I Cor. XI: 23-26, Mark XIV: 22-25, Matt. XXVI: 26-29 and Luke XXII: 17-20, in that order of date. We may note, in passing, that it is significant that the earliest account we have is found not in a Gospel but in an Epistle, and that it was written to resolve disputes which had already arisen concerning matters of administration—a proof, surely, of the hold which the Supper had obtained on the infant Church in the first twenty-five years after Christ's death. If we unite all these passages we can, I think, deduce the following scheme of eight meanings:—

Meanings.	*Scriptural Authority.*
I. In respect of the *Past.*	
1. The Sacrament is a memorial feast.	"This do in remembrance of Me." I Cor. XI. 24.
II. In respect of the *Present.*	
Individual.	
2. It is a method of teaching truth by symbol.	"This is My Body . . . this is My Blood." Mark XIV. 22, 24.
3. It is a sacrificial feast.	"My Blood . . . which is shed for many unto remission of sins." Matt. XXVI. 28.
4. It is the sign of a fixed agreement.	"This cup is the new Covenant (agreement) in My Blood." I Cor. XI. 25.
Social.	
5. It is the chief thanksgiving Service of the Church.	"When He had given thanks, He brake it." I Cor. XI. 24.
6. It is the family meal of the Church.	"He sat down and the twelve apostles with him." Luke XXII. 14.
7. It is the public sign of Christian discipleship.	"Where is the guest chamber, where I shall eat the passover with my disciples?" Luke XXII. 11. "He then, having received the sop, went immediately out: and it was night." John XIII. 30.

III. In respect of the *Future.*

    8. It is the prophecy of the perfected kingdom.   "Ye proclaim the Lord's death till He come."
                                      I Cor. XI. 26.

Two points, suggested by this scheme, catch the attention at once. (1) The Sacrament has chiefly to do with the *present.* One meaning touches the past: one looks into the future: but *six* have to do with the present. The Scripture seems to be heavily against those who see in it only an act of memorial. And (2) it affects equally the individual and the Christian community. This reacts on the question, to be discussed later, of the proper mode or modes in which the Sacrament should be celebrated.

III.

Now that we have stated our scheme of meanings, let us examine its component parts separately, that we may perceive the varying *weight* of its different elements,—an important matter, if we are to understand the Sacrament aright.

1. The Sacrament is a *Memorial Feast.* It is an occasion designed to keep alive a memory:

and, therefore, is a member of the class of "monumental" feasts, which includes secular, as well as sacred, celebrations. It is quite a common thing in colleges and schools to have a "Founder's day," on which the main festivity is the "Founder's feast." At these gatherings, it is customary to stand in silence, for a brief space, in honour of the benefactor, whose munificence gave birth to the college. The Lord's Supper is, in the first instance, a memorial of that sort. It is the Founder's feast of the Christian Church; and its simplicity makes it singularly apt for its purpose. The contrast between its beauty unadorned and the elaborate magnificence of corresponding secular banquets makes it all the more effective. A seemly memorial, this, for the Meek and Lowly, whose dream was "born in a herdsman's shed."

But while this meaning is true and authentic, it is the meaning which lies most obviously on the surface: and it is more than a pity that it has come to be regarded as the sole import of the Sacrament by so many people. This is but the starting-point, from which we proceed to the significances which are truly significant. Wherefore, we move on to remind ourselves that—

2. The Sacrament is *a Method of Teaching Truth by Symbol.* The use of symbol is important for the Reformed Churches. We have far too little of it. The banishment of the cross from our buildings, and especially from our Communion Tables, has impoverished us. Many a minister has wished that he could sometimes stop his sermon and, holding up a crucifix before his people, tell them to look and preach to themselves. Even so stalwart a defender of simple practice as the late Dr. Denny once gave expression to a desire of that sort. It may be true that our fathers regarded symbols as fit only for children—but they forgot that that is precisely what we are. It is to be hoped that the years ahead will see the increasing use of symbolic art and practice amongst us: but, meantime, we are authorized by Scripture to retain two purely symbolic services, namely, the Sacraments; and we must make the most of them.

It only needs a cursory glance at the symbolism of the Supper to see that it sets forth the heart of the Christian system. The benevolence of God is suggested by the fact that the Table is spread for us, and that on it He sets gifts, whose sole purpose is to sustain life. Our dependence upon God is indicated by our share in the Supper: for all that we have to do is to *take*. The historic Life and Death, by which the love of God is seen "visibly in the world at war with sin," are, of course, directly signified: but, in addition, the principles, which are proclaimed by the Life and Death, are shown through the symbols as well. For if the Bread and Wine declare anything, they declare the principle of "life from life through pain and death"—which is the condition of all progress. If we allow the mind to dwell for a while on the processes by which both bread and wine become agents to sustain life, we begin to perceive how eloquent and how deep their symbolism is. For, once, the bread was the seed, which had to lie buried in the ground, before it became first the blade, then the ear, then the full corn in the ear. When it reached its golden maturity, the sickle was laid to its stalk, and after it had been harvested and garnered, it was first ground into meal and then baked on the fire, before it was ready to change its life into new life in the bodies of men. A deeper parallel to the processes by which spiritual nourishment is communicated can hardly be conceived, except it be in the case of the wine, which

is also set on the Table. For, once, that wine
was the life-blood of some living clusters that
hung on a vine. Lowly, on the rocky hill-sides,
the vine-trees grow, pruned continually with
sharp knives that they may bring forth more
fruit. Even their little time of beauty is denied
them, for as soon as the grapes come to their
purple fulness, they are plucked' and flung into
the wine-press, where, literally, they are trodden
under the foot of man; thus becoming fit to fill
the Cup, and to be used to slake man's thirst.
After the same manner also is conveyed to man's
spirit the "wine of the soul in mercy shed." The
parallelism is arresting and complete.

All this, and much more, is taught by the
Sacrament, and it is taught in *silence*. For once,
the human voice is stilled: the "arguments about
it and about" are stayed: and God's own elo-
quence has a chance to be heard. No wonder
that an instructed people place much weight on
so great an opportunity to learn.

3. Next, the Sacrament is *a Sacrificial Feast*.
Doubtless, ideas connected with feasts of this
sort belong to the morning twilight of religion.
We no longer conceive of God as a Being who
requires to be appeased; or imagine that in par-

taking of the body of a victim, sacrificed to Him,
we shall obtain the benefits which that victim
was sacrificed to secure. But, from these early
half-thoughts about God and His ways with men,
certain ideas that are permanently valuable are
derived, and embodied in the symbolism of the
Sacrament. We are reminded, in particular,
that there are certain benefits which cannot be
earned, but always must come to us in the form
of gifts, pure and simple. Among these, forgiveness stands preëminent: and as, around the
Table, we eat the bread and drink the wine, we
remind ourselves not only that forgiveness is
there to take, and that it is as a gift, and not as
a right, that we must receive it, but that it is a
gift which always costs something to the Giver.
This fundamental, moral fact ought to be acknowledged by us all, and the idea that, by any
amount of suffering or endurance of penalty, we
can square accounts with God, should be put out
of our minds. The tragedy of sin is that it leaves
an effect which no subsequent obedience can
obliterate: for it jars the relation between the
sinner and the person sinned against, and the old
relation can never be restored. Imagine a young
wife, who thinks her husband to be the incar-

nation of all the knightly virtues, suddenly discovering him in some particularly mean lie. She may forgive him. He may repent, and live chivalrously ever after. A new, and very tender relation between them may be established, but it will be different from the old one: and the process of forgiveness, which involves endurance of the "jar" and readjustment to the new relation, obviously involves pain. In the same way, we have jarred relations with God: and, if forgiveness is to be ours, it must be a gift from Him—a gift which spells pain in the giving. All this, also, is symbolized in the Supper: which should stir us to yield the only return to God, which it is in our power to render—namely, to receive without hesitation or question, the amazing boon of His pardon. We can do nothing but take: but that we can do. "What shall I render unto the Lord for all His benefits toward me? I will take the Cup of Salvation."

4. In the fourth place, *the Sacrament is a Sign of a Fixed Agreement.* This meaning I hold to be the heart of the Sacrament, and ministers should give much pains to making it plain to their young communicants. In so doing, they should avoid all technical and archaic terms, and

endeavor to put it in language that will make it
a living idea to their hearts. It will not be necessary to say much about "covenant meals," except
to indicate that the Lord's Supper, related as
it was to the Passover, falls into the class—a
class of meal, in which an agreement between
two contracting parties was finally ratified and
sealed. As we teach, we can draw parallels, accurate enough, between partaking in a meal of
this sort and signing a "scrap of paper," according to our modern custom. In the Sacrament, two persons are fixing an agreement, the
terms of which are already arranged: and these
two persons are none other than the individual
communicant and God Himself. The important
point to emphasize is that *both* are contracting.
We are making our promises without doubt: but
so is God. If we can believe that, and live on the
belief, every Sacrament will be, in truth, a singular medicine for our sick souls.

Now, it is of manifest importance that we
should be clear and accurate as to the mutual
terms of a covenant of this kind. The benefits
of Communion may be lessened, or the Table
may be avoided altogether, if we overstate the
moral obligations involved for us, or understate

the promise given by God. Young communicants nearly always have a wrong idea of the responsibilities which they undertake when they "come forward." Consequently, we must be at pains to reassure them that God never asks anything beyond their powers, and that the main point of the sacramental act is not to remind them what they must do for God, but what God will do for them. On the one hand, we sign a double agreement involving (a) a *purpose* of discipleship, and giving (b) a *promise* of search for aid: on the other hand, God gives a *promise* of the granting of aid sufficient to see us through anything that may come to us in the way of trial or temptation. It is important, I think, to distinguish between the statement of purpose and the promise, on our side of the bargain. We cannot *promise* perfect discipleship. Next month, next year—who knows what sort of follies we shall commit? Who is prepared to say he will not lose his temper in August, or will do his whole duty all through February? But we *can* say that, as far as we know our own hearts, our life-purpose is to be Christ's disciples, and that if we sin it will be "not with our consenting." And, further, we can *promise* always to seek God's help. That is entirely within the range of our wills. I cannot say "I shall be perfectly sweet-tempered and entirely diligent this day next year"; but I can promise "I will ask for the divine help this day next year." Thereby, the right use of the day is made much more probable. At any rate, an agreement of that kind is one which we both can and ought to make; and, having made it, we can throw all our attention on to the divine promise, that the aid that is sought for will be forthcoming. It is this thought that makes the Communion so living and wonderful an act. It takes us away from our poor weakness, and flings us on to the strength of the Almighty: and it becomes richer and more wonderful still, as the years prove to us that God's promise of aid is a promise that is kept.

5. Turning now to the communal meanings of the Sacrament, we find that it is *the Chief Thanksgiving Occasion of the Church.* Ministers, who are responsible for the actual celebration, should have this in their minds, when arranging the hymns in the earlier part of the service, and when thinking over their prayers. A real effort must be made to get away from the

idea that it is a funeral service. It is, in point of fact, the precise opposite—it is an occasion of Communion with the Risen and ever-Living Lord. I have even heard ministers declare that they felt it to be out of harmony with Easter Day! Such is the effect of regarding it solely as a Memorial service. Anglicans are, of course, perfectly right in emphasizing Communion at Easter, when the thought of life as the outcome of death is especially in our minds. We must try to make it the most hopeful of all our times of worship, when we forget ourselves and our failures, and look altogether to Him who turneth the shadow into the morning. And, as our minds move towards Him, and we remember all that He does for us, the note of thanksgiving will naturally be heard on all our lips.

6. Further, the Sacrament is *the Family Meal of the Church*. It expresses the unity of the Christian society, in which every member draws his life from a common source: and indicates the consequent responsibilities of brotherhood. The ethical implications are wide and far-reaching. It is a constant rebuke to malice and all uncharitableness, and to the lesser, but equally ugly, meannesses of snobbery and petty

jealousy. We might imagine that a seat at the Table was the seat which would be most coveted by those who long for social betterment. Where will they find the spirit of the ideal society better suggested?

7. That attendance at the Sacrament is *a Badge of Christian Discipleship* will be denied by nobody. On the night of Institution the traitor went away, and only Christ's friends remained: and, ever since, participation in it has been a sign, to all whom it may concern, that communicants are on Christ's side. "I wanted to come forrit, for it was the last thing He askit o' His *freen's*" sobbed the girl in Ian Maclaren's story. No wonder that this aspect of the act is dwelt upon by sincere young communicants, and that it often makes them hesitate. "I am afraid that it will be a fraud"—how often have ministers heard fears like that from some of the best of catechumens. And, indeed, such fears are justified, for, at the Sacrament we don the knightly armour of Christ's Round Table. But we may call to our remembrance that no one goes on this warfare at his own charges; and, if the responsibilities of discipleship frighten us, we can take the mind back to the earlier word,

that tells us of a covenant of aid made with us by God. And in the hope which He inspires, we can enter, or reënter, the lists.

8. And, finally, the Sacrament is *a Prophecy of the Perfected Kingdom.* As it has its roots in the past, so it throws its beams into the future. It is the place for the dreamer, and for all to whom has come the heavenly vision. For it speaks of the far-off Divine event in whose consummation we may share and for which our work even now is effective. And because it is a Communion with the Living Lord, it is also a Communion with all those who live in Him. Our own dear and blessed dead are not far from us at the Table: and we obtain there a presage and surmise of the gladness of rejoicing that God intends for us, on the farther shore, some summer morning. If the Sacrament begins with the memory of love's dark ravine of sorrow, it ends with a vision of the land of pure delight. As we leave the Table, God's final word, clear and gracious, is "I bid you to hope."

IV.

One further point remains to be made, and it is of cardinal importance. The benefits of the

Sacrament are *inevitably* received by every communicant who participates sincerely and receptively. A spiritual process of strengthening runs parallel to the physical process of partaking,—provided the communicant is not eating and drinking unworthily. If a man comes to the Table carelessly, casually, frivolously; if he does not mean serious, spiritual business; if he is living against his own light and is impenitent; if he does not believe in spiritual help, nor attempt to be receptive of it—then he will gain nothing from the Communion, except harm. Nor are the benefits necessarily marked by any rise in the recipient's spiritual temperature. He may leave the Table feeling life as hard as when he came. But, nevertheless, he will of necessity be a stronger man: for this kind of aid usually comes without observation. When we have been ill, and are sent away to the mountains, or the sea, it is often quite a while before we feel physical invigoration. For days we may be as listless and languid as before. But we are breathing God's fresh air and bathing in God's sunshine—and, unfelt by ourselves, our bodies are recovering their tone, until, in due time, we are able to take up life's burdens again. The parallel between the physical and the spiritual world is often exact and illuminating. No sincere, penitent and strength-seeking soul ever partook in faith of the Sacrament without being strengthened with might by God's spirit in the inner man. Not, indeed, that there is any magical power possessed by the "creaturely elements." They remain bread and wine, and nothing else. But they become the physical agents by which spiritual thoughts, and thus spiritual forces, are let loose in the mind. The physical is the necessary servant of the spiritual—except, it may be, in the moments of pure illumination, which the mystics achieve. Even the influence of the Word is mediated by the physical. We need the printed page, communicated by light-rays to the optic nerve and thence to the brain, before ideas, which can liberate our wills, penetrate to the mind. Similarly, the bread and wine are the agents whereby the mind is so stirred that we may, in spiritual wise, partake of the Body and Blood of Christ. But, if they are rightly used, the communication of spiritual power is bound to be secured. We have nothing to do with its movement into our hearts. That is God's business. And that is why the Sacrament is an occasion of so great rest and so great hope. It is not, indeed, the only means of grace. God uses the Word, or sickness, or bereavement, or human love, to communicate His strength. But of all ordinary means of grace it is the chief.

CHAPTER VII.

THE CELEBRATION OF THE SACRAMENT.

WHAT, then, are we to do with an act of worship so full of the vital spark as this? How can we best use a gift so rich and rare? The Church has given various answers; but we may question whether any of our practices are wholly satisfactory. We are confined, of course, within the Reformed tradition, and that development of the Supper into "the drama of divine love and sorrow" called the Mass is beyond our purview. But, even in our branches of the Church, variations of practice have been considerable; and our immediate business is to discuss these to see if we cannot come to a greater uniformity, or, at least, agree upon the limits within which variations are desirable.

I.

(a) The first question that presents itself is as to the *frequency* of celebration. What we may call the Highland Presbyterian and the Anglican tradition stand at opposite poles in this respect. For the Anglican, the Table is always ready; for the Highland Presbyterian, it is spread, at most, twice a year. Which of these is more likely to secure the benefits of Communion?

The difficulty of giving an unequivocal answer is due to the fact, emphasized in the previous chapter, that the Sacrament is both individual and communal in its meaning. If we are to emphasize the latter aspect, celebration should not be frequent; if the former, it should be as frequent as possible. It is curious, by the way, to observe that the Presbyterian * practice is much more *churchly* than the Anglican. We shall have occasion to glance at this difference again in a moment or two; and here we simply note it to be a fact. If the Presbyterian use is to be followed, rarity is essential: for great public ceremonials, intended to express the common life of a society, lose their vitality and power of impact, if they come at too brief intervals. The modern habit of having Communion, after our manner, as often as once a month seems to me the worst

* Congregationalists and other friends will forgive the ecclesiastical adjective. I use it for convenience and "as in private duty bound."

possible of compromises. It is not nearly frequent enough to meet individual needs, and is too frequent to keep impressiveness as a Church festival.

(b) The *manner* of celebration is also a difficulty, arising from the same source. The Anglican mode, whereby each communicant advances to the altar and receives the elements separately, emphasizes the individual meaning: while the Presbyterian mode, in which the whole of the membership remains seated, as if around a common Table, and is served by elders, suggests especially the communal aspect of the Supper. Which of these is better—for both are right? If we can have only one, the question as to which should be retained provides a nice problem.

But is it necessary to make a choice? Cannot both be retained? The solution, I think, is to have great churchly Communions very rarely— probably not oftener than twice a year, and at these to use the Presbyterian mode: and to have very frequent Communions, in which the individual aspect is emphasized, either before the morning or after the evening service, and at these to use the Anglican mode. We do not want to weaken the dignified strength of the great sacramental seasons: but there is no good reason for depriving struggling souls of any help they can get from the Table, by never having it prepared for them when they need it. So, why not combine both methods, in the way suggested above?

No one who has ever seen a Communion Service in a great Scottish church will ever want to see the practice lost, or in any way cheapened by being made ordinary. One piece of symbolism, in frequent use in Scotland, is not, I think, copied on the Western side of the Atlantic. In the churches of the Old Land, the pews are provided with book-boards, and these, in addition to the Communion Table, are covered with white cloths specially made to fit them—or, at least, those attached to pews in which communicants are to sit. Intending participants take their places at the beginning of morning worship, thereby avoiding the unseemly shifting of seats, that sometimes occurs immediately before the celebration proper. The sight of a church thus covered in white is singularly impressive. Each child is sitting at His Father's board—each in his own place—each an indispensable member of the great family. When, amid the stillness, the bread and the cup are handed from one to another, the sense of the brotherhood of the Church is sometimes extraordinarily vivid. It is inconceivable that a practice so rich in meaning should be given up. But clearly, its power depends in part on its rarity: if for no other reason than that infrequency brings out a large proportion of the members. Communion of this sort should be attended by the whole available membership. In the old days, these occasions were surrounded by auxiliary services. From Thursday to Monday the community went into retreat: business came to standstill: each day became a Sabbath. It is, doubtless, impossible, even if it were desirable, to return to these practices: but, it is not impossible, if Communions of this kind occur only twice a year, to precede them with a week of special evening meetings. Modern communities need to go into retreat at least as badly as those of former generations—a need which is acknowledged in the development of services during Holy Week. It may reasonably be contended that the Communion would not only gain in significance, if this were done; but that the membership of the Church would rapidly incline to keep the preceding week free to attend preparatory services— to the great gain of everybody concerned.

And what is there in our principles which prevents us from affording frequent opportunities for individuals to covenant? There is a temperament which is particularly susceptible to symbol, and eager for sacramental worship. There is no reason, at all, that I can see, why we should force these into the fellowship of other Churches, by denying them help which the Communion is specially designed to afford. It is quite a simple thing to arrange a small room as a chapel, and to allow any member, who is in need, quickly to come and throw himself anew on God's promise of aid. If, on these occasions, we adopt the Anglican mode, we are not only making the act more effective from the individual point of view, but we are doing something, perhaps, to build a bridge over the gulf which separates us—for the perpetuation of our unfortunate divisions is due to differences in forms of worship, to a greater degree than we imagine. At any rate, it is a suggestion worth considering. As things are, we lose by not meeting the individual's sudden need or desire. A friend, who has adopted the double practice, tells me that he has found that young men, who had given up attendance at the stated Communions, avail themselves of the quieter and more private occasions. On the other hand, I am sure the Anglicans lose by never having great churchly celebrations of our type. Is it too much to hope that we may learn from one another?

(c) A third problem lies in the determination of those who shall come to the Communion. Too great ease and too great difficulty of access are both evils. Scotsmen know how hesitatingly the Highlander approaches the Table. He has got it into his head that only the elect may dare to lift the sacred emblems. His deep-seated reverence, and the spirit of fearfulness engendered among the mountains and the mists, hold him back. He is slow to believe that the gifts are there for sinners to take. His attitude, however, is greatly to be preferred to the heedlessness which sets the privilege free to anybody, anywhere and at any time. I have heard (but find it difficult to credit) than in some of our churches the Sacrament is given to children of very tender years, who have made no profession of faith. The only possible justification for a practice of this sort would be a belief in transubstantiation. It is done, I understand, in Roman churches logically enough: but that it should obtain in churches that pride themselves on their modern liberalism only shows how little the evangelic meaning of the Sacrament is understood. Participation in Communion should be the pledge of discipleship; and, consequently, it should not be encouraged too early. Children, of course, develop very differently: but, on the average, the age of sixteen is young enough. A catechumen ought to be sufficiently old to realize the moral struggle and to appreciate the reality of religion: and young children have not sufficient "years of discretion" for that. The period of later adolescence, between sixteen and twenty-one years of age, seems to be the appointed time.

The question of the moral qualifications for communicating is far more difficult. In old days, the Table was "fenced": indeed, it still is, in some places. A barrier was placed round it against heretics and sinners: and the authority for the practice was found in Scripture. St. Paul is clear as to the dangers of "eating and drinking unworthily." Perhaps the distinction may be put this way—those who are in sober earnest about breaking from sin should come: while those who are content to go on sinning should stay away. God offers help to those who are sufficiently in earnest to help themselves. If we come to *co-*

operate with God, then we are welcome. If we
come purely sentimentally, or on the off-chance
that some spiritual electric-shock will strike us,
whereby we shall find it easy to be good ever
after, we had better stay away. The Table is
spread for sinners unquestionably: but they must
be sinners who would be made whole. It is not
sin, but contentment in sin, that is the barrier.
Penitence and the stirring of hunger and thirst
after freedom take the fence away: and we,
fallen, baffled, tattered, ashamed, are called to
the place of God's refreshing and to the Table of
His love.

II.

Considerations such as these make it clear how
important it is to give instruction about the Sacrament, before young communicants are admitted. It is sometimes difficult to get them to
attend classes; but every effort should be made
to secure the coöperation of parents and teachers
that they may be encouraged to come. A gather-
ing once a week for at least four weeks, prior to
admission, is a minimum: and, if the minister can
manage it, he should see each catechumen pri-
vately as well. It may be that the scheme of

meanings in the previous chapter will be found useful for communicants' classes. At any rate, some carefully thought-out plan of instruction must be discovered, and only in rare and special cases should anyone be admitted who has not been taught in detail. Ignorance is the main danger of Christianity: and if members of the Church are ignorant of their own chief act of worship, the condition of the Church is perilous indeed.

It is not at all a bad plan to turn the whole congregation into a communicants' class every now and then. Two Sunday mornings every year spent on the meanings of the Sacrament are profitably used. Thereby, young communicants are reached: and their seniors are reminded of what they may have forgotten. Every minister, of course, must devise his own means for educating his congregation; but none of us should ever forget that steady and painstaking teaching is the unvarying condition of effective sacramental seasons.

III.

The actual celebration of Holy Communion should aim at two things—simplicity and silence.

No pains are too great to secure that all shall be done decently and in order. The minister will study the historic prayers of the Communion, and will watch that he omits no element—never forgetting the prayer of consecration before he administers. Minister and elders together will think out every arrangement, with the utmost care—if necessary, they will practise together—so that there will be no hitches or whispered consultations during the service itself. I once was at a Communion, the discomfort of which is in my mind to this day. The office-bearers became confused, and began to call to each other from opposite aisles to send cups or platters here or there. It made you feel ashamed—and all for the lack of preparation. When new churches are built, architects should be invited to consider the necessity of aisles so placed that the carrying of the bread and wine will be easy. Incidentally, all such churches will have a Communion Table and a Font as permanent furnishings. In our older churches, these are brought in as the occasion demands, with the result that, on an ordinary day, there is nothing to suggest that such churches are Christian temples. They are merely meeting-houses, with no indication of what sect or society uses them.

The practical problems of celebration have been increased by the modern innovation of the individual cups. I suppose it is too late to protest against them. Once this hygienic microbe gets into our mental systems, there is no stopping it: but one is inclined to enquire whether insurance companies ask higher premiums from Roman Catholics and Anglicans than they do, say, from Congregationalists. It would be scientifically interesting to discover whether there is an appreciably higher rate of mortality in their membership, which can be reasonably traced to their use of the common cup. When a man remembers the stately stillness of some older Communions, he wishes he did not live in so enlightened, so progressive and (let us add) so jumpy an age. However, as I say, the thing is past praying for. But we must realize that thereby our difficulties in securing stillness and smoothness in administration are increased. The tinkle of the cups: the contortions of those who drink from them: the return of trays to their appointed place—all these detract from the ordered quiet, which means so much. Many must have found it necessary, as I have done, to ask the organist to play softly during the passage of the cups: and that is a bad second best. I may add that, personally, I extremely dislike the plan whereby the communicants hold the bread and wine until all have been served and then partake at the same moment. It cuts at the root of the solitary covenant—which is so important a meaning of the Sacrament. For the rest, we must do the best we can; it will not be so bad for those who have never known anything better.

The common cup, however, should always be on the Communion Table, and the minister should use it when reading the Scripture warrant. Seeing that the whole Sacrament is a symbolism, he should be very careful about all the symbolic acts. An unbroken slice of bread should be ready to his hand, which he will break in the sight of the people; he should lift the Cup high when he utters the words "this cup is the new covenant in my blood." These little things add so much. Nothing is too slight or too immaterial to be negligible. Every arrangement, every detail should be given all the reverent care at our command; for the Supper may be the simplest meal in the world, but it is a Supper with the King.

CHAPTER VIII.

THE GUIDANCE OF THE WISE.

ONE of the most charming pictures that comes down to us from long ago is that of a certain chubby little monk sitting smiling "in his little corner with his little book." For the monk was Thomas à Kempis: and if his "little book" could make that master of sorrows smile, it had proved that literature helps us "to enjoy life or to endure it," before Dr. Johnson thus phrased its purposes. As we conclude these studies, let us follow the old monk's example and retire into a corner with a book or two, not that we may either enjoy life or endure it, but that we may obtain guidance from the wise as to how we should bear ourselves as ministers. The sages of many generations are ready and waiting to help us: and if ever men needed help, we are those men. Wherefore, let us take down a few of their volumes from our shelves, and, as we turn the pages, let them speak to us, who have the right.

1. *The Call to the Ministry.*

And first let us ask ourselves whether we have any right to be in the ministry at all. Is there any infallible mark or sign of the selected man? Well, I think we can get one valuable hint in this *obiter dictum* of Principal Dykes,—"The noblest passion, that can beat in the heart of a man, is the passion to deliver." A man who would be a minister is one who has been caught by that high enthusiasm, and who gives himself no peace unless he is doing something to help the helpless. The clamant need of men for healing, and the desire to satisfy it, stir him continually to an urgent restlessness.

> "I slumber not—the thorn is in my couch,
> Each day a trumpet soundeth in my ear,
> Its echo in my heart."

As a result, he gives willing assent to the famous utterance of F. W. H. Myers, "Remember, that, first of all, a man must, from the torpor of a foul tranquility, have his soul delivered unto war." And, as far as he knows his own heart, he must be able to say that the longing to deliver has caught him for good. "It is not the strength, but the duration, of great sentiments," says Nietszche, "that maketh great men." The quality of adherence, which Browning calls devotedness ("devotedness, in short, which I account the ultimate in man") is as necessary as enthusiasm. Other characteristics, doubtless, are desirable before a man becomes a leader in worship: but if he can honestly say that, as far as he understands himself, he is devoted to the task of deliverance, he has one good ground, at any rate, for believing that his call to the ministry is authentic.

2. *The Minister as a Friend.*

People are only delivered, as a rule,.by those that love them. In the Christian realm this is always true. Jesus was a Saviour, because He was a friend of publicans and sinners. Wherefore, a minister will cultivate his genius for friendship, and thank God for its possession. It is a curious as well as a supreme gift: and I know not what can be rightly said about it. You never can say much about hidden things like friendship, for they defy analysis. You can simply know them and give God the praise. But this, at least, we affirm—friendship cannot dwell with scorn. Wherefore, a minister will cleanse his heart and mind of all that is disdainful of any of his people. He must have his eyes open to their nobility. He

must respect them.   He must see the kingly in
them.   Indeed, he has good reason so to do: for
God lives in them all, especially, perhaps, in the
inconspicuous and the drab.   Mr. Noyes sings it
worthily.

> "Leaders unknown of hopes forlorn
> Go past us in the daily mart,
> With many a shadow crown of thorn
> And many a kingly broken heart."

We shall, therefore, keep free from all censorious,
critical, contemptuous thoughts of our people, as
far as in us lies, knowing that disdain is the eldest
daughter of the Queen of Sins.   Robert Bridges
has a good word when he writes—

> "Earth hath no sin but thine
> Dull eye of scorn:
> O'er thee the sun doth pine,
> And angels mourn."

If our people act unworthily, we shall try to pity
them as a doctor pities a sick child.   And if they
act meanly to us, let us keep in our hearts this
wisdom from William Blake, "Friendship cannot
exist without the forgiveness of sins continually."
Moreover, we must rejoice greatly in their affection for us and keep it as a treasure and a prize,
not forgetting that one of the most charming of
writers has said that, "The world has a million

roosts for a man, but only one nest." Oliver Wendell Holmes would be the first to agree that a minister who found a nest among his people was a minister who had succeeded. For with the gift of friendship goes the gift of trust, and "To know someone we love believes in us is the finest incentive to becoming worthier of such a faith," as Richard King has it in his "Confessions of an Average Man." And, if trial comes to us, we may see in it a chance of the prize of learning friendship in its truth and depth. There is a fine old Scots proverb that is worth our pondering, "Nae man can be happy without a friend, nor sure of him till he's unhappy." At any rate, Jeremy Bentham was right when he said, "If you would gain mankind the best way is to appear to love them, and the best way of appearing to love them is to love them in reality." The chance to show that we love them will come best in their times of trouble,—concerning which a word of warning comes from Madagascar, where they have this admirable proverb, "Sorrow I can bear, but not the professional mourner." But, above all, let us reflect on this from George Macdonald,

"'Tis but as men draw nigh to Thee, My Lord,
They can draw nigh each other and not hurt."

3. *The Minister as a Leader.*

All ministers aspire to leadership in the community; more's the pity, sometimes. But, in the sphere of their own congregations they are called upon to lead, though without arrogance. Upon this matter let us set down, first, an admirable statement by that great Englishman, Lord Morley, who knew what leading meant. "The decisive sign of the elevation of a nation's life is to be sought among those who lead or ought to lead, and in the action of those whom it accepts or chooses to be its chiefs." The responsibility thrown on us, therefore, is severe. Leadership is greatly prized, especially in a democracy, where it is alleged to go not by favour, but by merit. In the ministry, however, it comes by virtue of a position; we are among those to whom much is given and from whom, consequently and reasonably, much is required. The "communal obligation," which goes so deep, is laid upon us: and, if we fail our people in matters of common rectitude, the memory will haunt us to the end of the journey. However many excuses they make for us, we shall never be able to excuse ourselves. For we shall be continually afraid that failure in

other lives is directly to be traced to our own.
Christina Rossetti expresses the inner anger of
many a minister's heart when she writes,

> "Clearly his own fault. Yet, I think,
> My fault in part, who did not pray
> But lagged and would not lead the way."

Moreover, ministerial leadership must never be
selfish. It must be leadership inspired by the
passion to deliver. Diotrephes, who loved the
preëminence, would have made the worst kind of
minister—although a kind that is painfully common. We need to listen to Miss Rossetti again,

> "Not to be first: how hard to learn
> That life-long lesson of the past,
> Line graven on line and stroke on stroke—
> But, thank God, learned at last."

These things are, of course, basal; and they are,
I make no doubt, clearly in our minds; and we
mean to achieve them by God's grace, which can
do marvelous things. But there are minor matters, which have their own importance, and are
more easily forgotten. The minor may be only
the major on a small scale. Courtesy, for instance, is an outgrowth of love: suffering fools, as
gladly as circumstances permit, is the natural
attitude of a man who desires to deliver: patience

with the unreasonable is the sign of a heart of
generous sympathy.   Wherefore, we may not
neglect the insignificant things of conduct, if we
aspire to leadership.   "It is the little things," Dr.
Dykes used to say, "that spoil most ministeries."
Take care of the pennies of gentleness and win-
someness, and the pounds of leadership will look
after themselves.   Thus, watch things like good
nature, tact ("tact is the gift of doing the right
thing in place of the obvious," remarks Mr. Shane
Leslie), and above all equanimity in controversy.
In "Penelope's Experiences in Scotland," Mrs.
Wiggin makes one of her characters describe a
friend as being "very like that young man who,
whenever he engaged in controversy, seemed to
take off his flesh and sit in his nerves."   We all
know that youth, and how distressing he becomes
when he retains his unpleasant skill in undressing
into later years.   It is, of course, inevitable that
we shall be engaged in disputes: and a really
great ecclesiastical controversy is a most exhil-
arating thing.   But it must be kept on a high
level.   The lesser disputes, into which we are
sometimes dragged, are not only unnecessary, but
indecent; and would never develop if we only
kept our flesh over our nerves.   After all, "what

can be more honourable to a man than to be
charged with an excess of good-nature," as John
Firth gives it in his translation of the Younger
Pliny. And as far as our own congregation is
concerned, let us take to heart Tennyson's line,
"The King who fights his people, fights himself."
But the main point about leadership is that it
should be *leadership*. The leader should be in the
van,—ahead of his people in belief, in hope, in
energy. The remark of Dr. Whyte who was
endeavouring to revitalize the congregational
prayer-meeting, which had become somewhat
half-hearted, is worth calling to mind: "I put a
lot of steam into it," he said. At any rate, let
there be clearly written, where it can be seen
every day, this reflection from "The Road to
Rannoch" by Dr. Barnett, "The true principle
of sport may be summed up in the words, Do it
yourself."

4. *The Minister and Things Marginal.*

In this matter of being a leader, or a pastor, or
a preacher, or just a man, we shall often be faced
by things marginal. Irritating, perplexing, per-
turbing things they are. By them I mean all
those practices, habits, attitudes or indulgences

which are legitimate, but not always expedient.
And in respect of them, let us be commended to
the god of common sense, of whom we all stand
in need: some of us, alas! more than others. That
they are permissible, and even useful, is suggested
by William Pitt's outburst, "Don't tell me of a
man's being able to talk sense. Every one can
talk sense; can he talk nonsense?" And Mr.
Shane Leslie carries the matter further when he
remarks, "Only the idealist continues to be an un-
dergraduate through life." But that here we are
dealing with a marginal area, in which it behooves us to walk circumspectly, is shown by Dr.
Johnson's attitude to the merriment of parsons.
We shall not be ill-guided if we go to three very
different men, who look at the thing from very
different angles. George Herbert, who was not
much troubled with the marginal, inclines to the
side of safety, which, I daresay, is the best side
for us all.

"Who keeps no guard upon himself is slack
And rots to nothing at the next great thaw."

Marcus Aurelius, also I should imagine a non-
marginal man, puts a familiar and very sound
principle freshly when he writes, "That which is
not good for the swarm neither is it good for the

bee." But the happiest, and the tenderest and the most sympathetic advice comes from Mr. G. K. Chesterton, who possibly knows more about margins than the other two. Says he, "Our wisdom, whether expressed in private or public, belongs to the world, but our folly belongs to those we love."

5. *The Minister in the Pulpit.*

But, after all, our main task is in the pulpit; and though we have spent some time considering some aspects of that matter, let us see if we can cull some flowerlets of wisdom upon it from the sages. Dr. John Ker (a man of genius, whose writings should be more widely known than they are) points out that "Preaching, or regular religious instruction, is peculiar to Christianity," and that within the church, "Protestantism, as compared with Romanism, is the religion of public speech." "The church," he adds, "that cannot and will not preach, and preach well, must go down." The fact is that in preaching a man is, in a particular way, meeting an obligation which is meant to be incumbent on all men. We owe the statement to Epictetus that "God has introduced man to be a spectator of God and His works: and

not only a spectator of them, but an interpreter."
Whether that is the function of all men or not, it
is certainly the function of the preacher. God
has, unquestionably, introduced him into the
world to be an interpreter. But because he is an
interpreter in a pulpit, his task is a hazardous one.
"The great danger of a platform orator's career
is that it may in time lessen a man's moral self-
possession," is Lord Morley's comment: and the
pulpit is not so far removed from the platform
that it can feel safe. Wherefore, we must be very
watchful about honesty. While we are careful to
distinguish between our prejudices and our principles, and to prevent the bee that buzzes in our
bonnets from buzzing in our sermons, we will
do well to remember our last-quoted authority
when he says, "He who begins life by stifling his
convictions is in a fair way to ending it with no
convictions to stifle." And with moral earnest-
ness and honestly we will place thought. Good
hard thinking, up to our conceivable height, is the
foundation-stone of every sermon that is worth
while. Charles Spurgeon phrased it pithily when
he wrote, "Weigh your sermons. Do not retail
them by the yard, but deal them out by the
pound." Along with all this we must try to sug-

gest a sense of mystery, and of our own inadequacy. So to do is, indeed, an aspect of honesty. "It was necessary," said Aquinas, "for certain things, to be proposed to man from God that altogether exceeded his understanding," and a due admission that we are not omniscient should be observable in our words and in our manner. And that word "manner" suggests many reflections. No man can compute the number of sermons that are spoiled in their setting-out: by gesture (try to suit the action to the word, or, for pity's sake, refrain from action), or by a queer, unnatural voice. "Moreover, brethren, avoid the use of the nose as an organ of speech, for the best authorities are agreed that it is intended to smell with." "Why speak so as to be heard in the street when there is nobody there who is listening to you?" Thus, with homely sense, counsels Spurgeon. Even clothes are not unimportant. Richard King somewhere remarks, "Clothes were evolved in order that many of us might look more impressive than we really are." On the other hand, ministerial garb, while adding impressiveness (if necessary), helps to sink the man in his office: and, anything that can do that is to be encouraged. But, to move upward a little to the matter of style, Schleiermacher has a good thing upon that when he says, "The speech of the pulpit should have for its basis the language of the Bible." Even if that advice needs some qualifications it is not bad advice for a young minister. A man, however, may be too careful about the form. "He who takes overmuch thought for his style is in danger of losing the way to excellence," comments Sir Edward Cook: and he adds, "When there is perfect sincerity, the art, however magnificent, is never visible—the passion and the truth hide it."   The main thing is to be simple and clear, remembering that simplicity and clarity are the friends, and not the enemies, of beauty. Victor Hugo's epigram that "The beautiful is as useful as the useful, perhaps more so," is as applicable to preaching as to anything else.   But these are not the chief matters.   What we have to seek most of all is the instinct of sympathy.   "I sat where they sat," claimed Ezekiel.   "Expose thyself to feel what wretches feel," advised Shakespeare.   Indeed, we do not need to expose ourselves.   We "ken by oorsel's." Honest dealing with our own painful need will bring an undertone of fellow-feeling into our sermons: and will save us from that talking down, as if from a lofty moral plane, which is at once useless and insincere. Tennyson's line, "It is better to fight for the good than to rail at the ill," gives a valuable hint for our pulpit work. It is to be hoped that, up to our measure, the same thing can be said about us as was said about Gladstone, "He knew men well enough, at least to have found out that none gains such an ascendance over them as he who appeals to what is the nobler part of human nature." And, with sympathy, let urgency go hand in hand. We should often quote to ourselves the familiar lines in Myers' "St. Paul" beginning—

"Oft when the Word is on me to deliver
    Lifts the illusion and the truth lies bare;
Desert or throng, the city or the river,
    Melts in a lucid Paradise of air,—"

But the whole secret of effective preaching is contained in the amazing compliment paid to John Brown of Haddington by David Hume, "That's the man for me, he means what he says: he speaks as if Jesus was at his elbow."

6. *The Minister as a Pilgrim.*

It is, I think, Mr. Housman who remarks in an introduction to some classical work that,

amidst all the perplexities of our earthly lot, one
point stands clear: "Life is no feather-bed for
sluggards to lie in." You remember how Sir
Walter Scott was delighted with the description
given of herself by an old beggar woman, "A'm
just an auld struggler." Stevenson has put the
same idea into Doric verse,—

> "My bonny man, the world it's true
> Was made for neither me nor you:
> It's just a place to warstle through."

And Francis Thompson, more lugubriously, has
reëchoed the Scriptural writer's opinion that man
is born to trouble as the sparks fly upwards,—

> "Nothing begins and nothing ends
> That is not paid with a moan;
> For we are born in other's pain
> And perish in our own."

Now, from this general fate ministers are not
exempt. On the contrary. To begin with, they
will probably be poor; economic conditions thereby coöperating with Providence to keep them
humble. They are likely to have a lot of irritating, peddling sort of work to do. They certainly
will have plenty of exercise in the wearisome art
of smoothing ruffled feathers. And, in addition,
they will have to look after themselves, remem-

bering that a city that is set on a hill cannot, alas!
be hid. Each profession, as a clever lady suggested, has its métier. "A soldier's métier is to
be brave: a solicitor's to be honest: and a minister's to be good." It is only another way of saying that a bishop's business is to be an example to
the flock and that he therefore has to be more
careful than the next man, especially if he be red-
blooded. There is no escape from the insistent
challenge of our métier. Even getting out of
clerical clothes, according to the (as I think)
rather regrettable custom of the New World,
will not deliver us. We are definitely faced with
a terribly testing life, and the only thing to do is
to face it, even if we feel that it involves restraints
that are unreasonable. After all, life's restric-
tions are God's will. We remember our Browning:—

> "We are in God's hand,
> How strange now looks the life He makes us lead;
> So free we seem, so fettered fast we are:
> I feel He laid the fetter, let it lie."

Moreover (for we may as well look at the worst
of it), it is just as well to realize that it is not at
the beginning that life's road-way blisters our
feet. "Morning never tries you till the afternoon," says Kipling. Still less does life unfold

its harshness in advance; which is the reason why he that putteth on his armour is more inclined to boast than he that putteth it off. "He's a grand man for an expedition *tomorrow*," is apt to be a true description of most of us. Dr. Barbour records that a young minister fresh from a conference on the deepening of spiritual life, once came into Dr. Whyte's study and spoke of his experiences with rapture, just as if the New Jerusalem had come. "Aye," said Dr. Whyte, "it's a sair fecht up to the very last." Well, there is nothing for it but to admit that life is a grave business. "To Rossetti," says Walter Pater, "life is a crisis at every moment. A sustained impressibility towards the mysterious conditions of man's everyday life, towards the very mystery itself in it, gives a singular gravity to all his work." This, at least, is one of the "treasures of darkness" we may mine from life's harshness. If it lends a "singular gravity" to our conduct of worship, our discipline will not have been unfruitful. After all, we may allow Marcus Aurelius to comfort us when he says that, "Nothing happens to any man which he is not found by nature to bear," and we may also remember that it *is* possible to "turn our necessities to glorious gain": it is

possible to be *more* than conquerors. We have
the unfailing witness of the saints to the good that
always resides in the heart of pain. And if our
trials be temptations, the same thought comes to
sustain:—

"Why comes temptation but for man to meet
And master and make crouch beneath his feet,
And so be pedestalled in triumph?"

Whatever happens, endure: and that without too
much introspection. Lady Gwendollen Cecil
tells us that her father, Lord Salisbury, "used to
quote with approval Kingsley's dictum, that a
man wins a boat-race by pulling hard and not by
stopping to feel his muscles." It is sound advice.
After all, we are not called upon to endure forever. So "stand up, stand up for Jesus: *the fight
will not be long.*" But, meantime, there is the
sound of battle and the alarm of war in these
wayward hearts of ours: let us respond as gal-
lantly as we can. Dr. Carroll in his commentaries
on Dante reminds us that, "To love the good
without fulfilling it in duty is to create within the
soul the night in which no man can work." I
once picked up an anonymous poem in an
English magazine, one verse of which has stuck

in my mind ever since. It suggests the true, knightly attitude, in all this business,

> "The world says, Promise little and no thought
> Of faith unfaithful holds you from your sleep.
> So rots the world. Nay, rather be it yours
> To promise greatly and your promise keep."

This is a word specially needed by ministers: and that we may heed it, let me give a piece of advice, —keep at your elbow a copy of the poems of that strange, strong woman, so "human at the red-ripe of the heart," Christina Rossetti, and pray some of her prayers after her. As, for instance, this:—

> "God harden me against myself,
> This coward with pathetic voice
> Who craves for ease, and rest, and joys."

And every now and then stretch out a hesitating hand to Richard Baxter, that terrible man, with his searchlight focused on our need. You remember the kind of warning he rings out, as thus: "Believe it, brethren, God never saved any man for being a preacher, nor because he was an able preacher; but because he was a justified, sanctified man, and consequently faithful in his Master's work." Or thus: "The work may be God's, and yet we may do it. not for God, but for ourselves. I confess I feel such continual danger on this point, that if I do not watch, lest I should study for myself, and preach for myself, and write for myself, rather than for Christ, I should soon miscarry." And turn back to Miss Rossetti again to find this comforting and satisfying dialogue between God and your soul,—

"Lord, carry me.—Nay; but I grant thee strength
To walk and work thy way to heaven at length."

A man has a chance of winning through, when at last and finally he leans back on God. "Human wisdom has reached its furthest point when it gets to say, I do not know—God knows," says Dr. Brown in the "Horae Subsecivae." And human power has reached its height when it says, "Lord I cannot, but Thou canst."

7. *The Minister as an Optimist.*

Someone has happily called the Apostle Paul the theologian of hope. He has, at any rate, struck out a significant phrase, when he speaks of "the hope that saves." This is the word that comes back to the world from Goethe's marching heroes: "We bid you," they cry, "to hope." Wherefore, let us make our mental companionship with those who have proved that victory cannot only be won, but can be splendid. Those are noble words, taken from a speech of his own to students, that are inscribed on Mr. Gladstone's tombstone in Hawarden Church: "Be inspired with the belief that life is a great and noble calling; not a mean and grovelling thing that we are to shuffle through as best we can, but an elevated and lofty destiny." And in his life he showed what a belief of that kind can do to inspire a man to works of noble note. The type of inner thought that he cultivated is displayed by an entry from his diary which his biographer permits himself to quote:—"In practice the great end is that the Love of God may become a habit of my soul, and particularly these things are to be sought:—1. The spirit of Love. 2. of self-sacrifice. 3. of purity. 4. of mercy." When we come to think of it, there is evidence and to spare that life *is* both elevated and lofty: and that, in the special work to which we are called, there is no such thing as ultimate defeat. There is pioneer work to be done, and pioneer work is hard, but (as Mr. Arthur Jose has it) :—

> "Each camp-fire has marked a spot
> That men shall call their home."

So take the road gaily with a gallant English
poet, Arthur Clough:—

"Go with the sun and the stars, and yet evermore in the
    Spirit,
Say to thyself, It is good, yet is there better than it.
This that I see is not all, and this that I do is but little:
Nevertheless it is good, though there is better than it."

So now we come to our conclusion, with four
quotations from very different sources. The first
two hint at the fulfilment of our work, and what
the outcome is to be when the chief Shepherd
shall appear. We know that we shall need "our
good and ill forgotten, and both forgiven by His
abounding grace;" but we may pray that, in this
world, the evil that we do may not live after us,
nor the good be interred with our bones. After
Cardinal Newman died, Miss Rossetti wrote a
poem on him, which ends with a prayer that we
may make for each other and for ourselves:—

"Now fixed and finished thine eternal plan.
    Thy best has done its best, thy worst its worst:
    Thy best its best, please God, thy best its best."

It was a Scottish poetess, writing from a Scottish
manse, who lifted up her eyes behind the veil, and
thought of what a man may feel, when he dis-
covers how he has been used of God for purposes
that stretch out into eternity. It was into the

mouth of Samuel Rutherford that she put the
sudden exclamation,—

> "Ah! if one soul from Anwoth
> Meet me at God's right hand,
> My heaven shall be two heavens
> In Immanuel's land."

Meantime our work lies before us; let us turn to
it with the inspiration of two sayings which touch
upon the heart of the matter, for they deal with
that inner enthusiasm of love without which no
man shall be a preacher, or a minister, or, indeed,
a true man at all. Of these, I take first a word
from Izaak Walton, that lover of gentle places
and gentle streams, and of the craft that sets the
sign of serenity in a man's eyes. He spoke of a
greater fishing than he imagined when he said,
"I am like to have a towardly scholar of you. I
now see that with advice and practice you will
make an angler in a short time. *Have but a love
of it, and I'll warrant you.*" But of all such sayings the one I like best comes from an English
dean of the last generation, who found his rest
and recreation in the growing of roses,—a seemly
practice, surely, for a worker in God's garden.
He has written a charming book on the culture
of his favourite flower,—the sort of book that

takes a man away from care and noise and battle, and sets him down in the midst of beauty and peace. And he begins his instruction with a sentence which I commend to all those who work for noble things,—

> "He that would have beautiful roses in his garden must have beautiful roses in his heart."